As per the New ICSE Syllabus

Science Panorama 8

Chemistry

Series Editor
Lipika Dutta

Collins

As per the New ICSE Syllabus

Science Panorama 8

Chemistry

Series Editor

Lipika Dutta

Published by Collins India
A division of HarperCollins*Publishers* India Private Limited

HarperCollins *Publishers*
A-75, Sector 57, Noida, Uttar Pradesh 201301, India
1 London Bridge Street, London SE1 9GF, United Kingdom
Hazelton Lanes, 55 Avenue Road, Suite 2900, Toronto, Ontario M5R 3L2
and 1995 Markham Road, Scarborough, Ontario M1B 5M8, Canada
25 Ryde Road, Pymble, Sydney, NSW 2073, Australia
195 Broadway, New York, NY 10007, USA

Browse the complete Collins catalogue at **www.collins.in**

First published in 2017

ISBN: 978-93-5264-3-479

Content developed by **ExcelSoft Technologies Pvt. Ltd.**

Artwork and layout by **Quadrum Solutions, Recto Graphics**

Printed and bound by Thomson Press

MRP: ₹ 317

Acknowledgements

Cover: dem10, iStockphoto

Title Page: dem10, iStockphoto

Inside: **Page 17**: Eky Studio, Gordana Sermek, Anan Kaewkhammul; **18**: Catmando; **19**: stockphoto mania; **21**: talseN; **23**: carlosalvarez; **24**: Arena Photo UK Alexandra Lande; **31**: Lakeview Images; **32**: discpicture; **35**: Xiebiyun; **36**: chemicalbilly, HTU; **44**: Georgios Kollidas; **88**: tusumaru; **95**: Owen Price, bdspn, Kalulu; **102**: EyeEmCLOSED; **105**: studioVin, hxdbzxy; **117**: royaltystockphoto, Boris25; **119**: Martin McCarthy; **120**: Leonid Andronov; **121**: SeDmi; **122**: stocksnapper; **123**: quadxeon; **129**: helendol, Jim DeLillo

Preface

Science Panorama is a series of books for Classes 1 to 8, which includes 3 books each for Physics, Chemistry and Biology for middle school. The middle school series has been updated based on the **new syllabus** prescribed by the **Council for the Indian School Certificate Examinations**. In line with the new syllabus, a thematic, coherent and structured approach has been followed and all the new topics suggested in the syllabus have been included. Chapter-wise worksheets have also been provided to effectively integrate subject knowledge and life skills for overall development.

This updated edition also emphasizes on developing scientific skills such as observation, investigation, analysis, research and other inferential skills. It focuses on development of concepts as well as their application in real life. Sufficient examples from everyday life have been provided to help learners understand the concepts using age-appropriate language. Colourful illustrations and well-labelled diagrams have been included to engage learners and aid their understanding.

Some Key Features

Science in Context: Additional information on the topic being taught

Do You Know? Interesting facts related to the given topic

Challenge Yourself: Questions testing students' ability to reason and extrapolate

Activities: Individual/collaborative activities to hone experimental and deduction skills

Know the Scientist: Famous scientists and their contribution to the topic at hand

Greenathon: Some tips to keep the environment clean and green

Revision Zone: In-text questions for assessing progress in the course of learning

Keywords: Important terms from the chapter along with their definitions

In a Nutshell: Summary of the chapter content

Exercise: Variety of questions given at the end of each chapter

Subject Integration Worksheets: To effectively integrate knowledge across subjects

Life Skills Worksheets: To create awareness, empathy and a positive attitude towards self and others

Assessment papers: Two assessment papers at the end of the book for effective evaluation

We would like to take this opportunity to thank all the teachers who reviewed the books and provided their valuable feedback, which helped in improving the quality of the content.

Any suggestions or constructive criticism from the users are welcome. We shall try to incorporate those in the future editions.

Authors

Key Features

Do You Know?

Interesting facts related to the given topic

Do You Know?

Pieces of pumice rocks can float on water. This is because the air pores in them make the stone less dense than water. This helps ...e stone to float for a ...s after a wh...

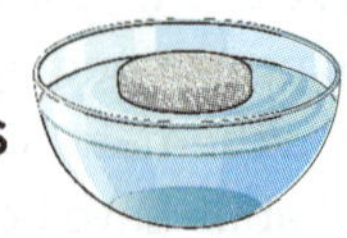

Science in Context

Additional information on the topic being taught

Science in Context

In a liquid and a gas, the molecules are loosely packed, so they have some regions with more molecules and other regions with fewer molecules. The movement ...f molecules from a region ...igher concentration t... ...lower con...

Challenge Yourself

Questions testing students' ability to reason and extrapolate

Challenge Yourself

You might have noticed that cut pieces of some vegetables and fruits like potato, apple, etc., turn brown when exposed to air if they are not consumed immediately. ... you know what kind of a... ... it is?

Know the Scientist

Famous scientists and their contribution to the topic at hand

Know the Scientist

Joseph Priestley (1733–1804) was an English chemist. He is credited for the isolation and discovery of oxygen in its gaseous state. He named it as 'dephlogisticated air'. He also synthesized nitrous oxide (laughing gas).

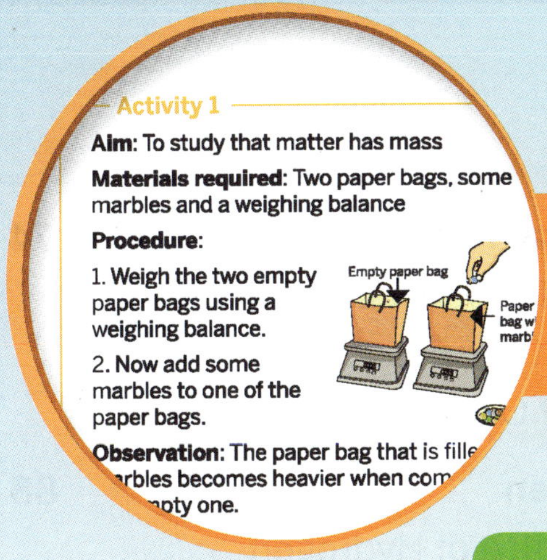

Activity 1

Aim: To study that matter has mass

Materials required: Two paper bags, some marbles and a weighing balance

Procedure:

1. Weigh the two empty paper bags using a weighing balance.
2. Now add some marbles to one of the paper bags.

Observation: The paper bag that is fille
arbles becomes heavier when com
pty one.

Activity

To hone experimental and deduction skills

Revision Zone

In-text questions for assessing progress

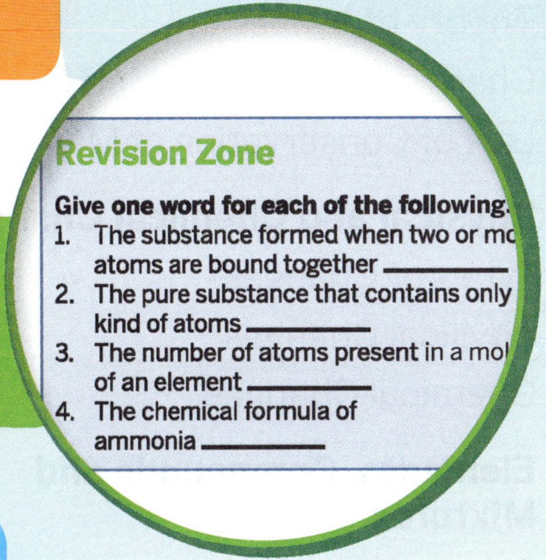

Revision Zone

Give one word for each of the following

1. The substance formed when two or mo atoms are bound together ______
2. The pure substance that contains only kind of atoms ______
3. The number of atoms present in a mol of an element ______
4. The chemical formula of ammonia ______

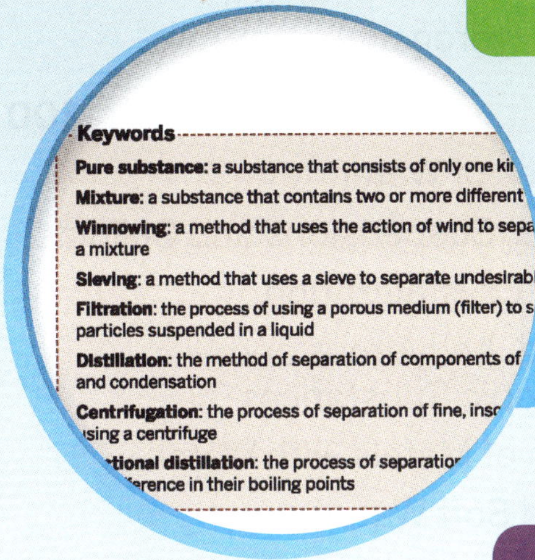

Keywords

Pure substance: a substance that consists of only one kin

Mixture: a substance that contains two or more different

Winnowing: a method that uses the action of wind to sepa a mixture

Sieving: a method that uses a sieve to separate undesirabl

Filtration: the process of using a porous medium (filter) to s particles suspended in a liquid

Distillation: the method of separation of components of and condensation

Centrifugation: the process of separation of fine, inso using a centrifuge

tional distillation: the process of separation ference in their boiling points

Keywords

Definitions of key terms from the chapter

Exercise

Variety of questions given at the end of each chapter

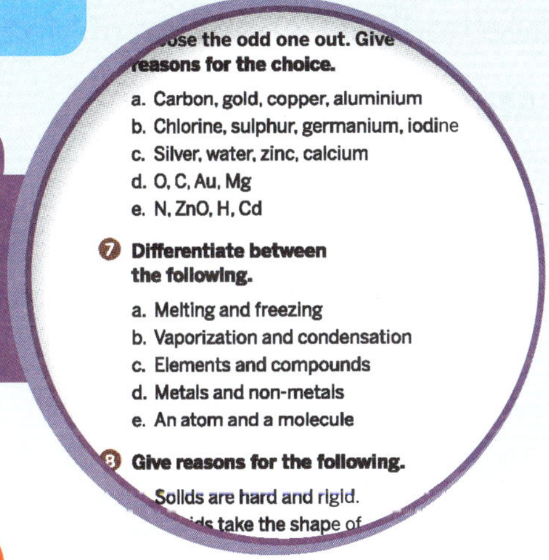

ose the odd one out. Give reasons for the choice.

a. Carbon, gold, copper, aluminium
b. Chlorine, sulphur, germanium, iodine
c. Silver, water, zinc, calcium
d. O, C, Au, Mg
e. N, ZnO, H, Cd

7. **Differentiate between the following.**

a. Melting and freezing
b. Vaporization and condensation
c. Elements and compounds
d. Metals and non-metals
e. An atom and a molecule

8. **Give reasons for the following.**

Solids are hard and rigid.
ids take the shape of

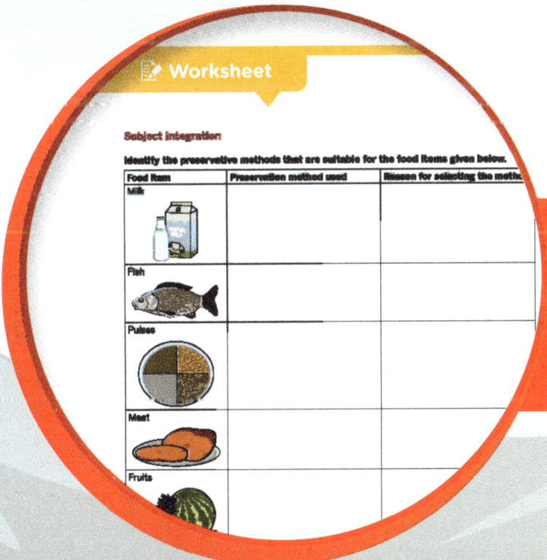

Worksheet

Subject integration

Identify the preservative methods that are suitable for the food items given below.

Food item	Preservation method used	Reason for selecting the metho
Milk		
Fish		
Pulses		
Meat		
Fruits		

Worksheet

Thematic worksheets on integration of knowledge across subjects and Life Skills

Contents

Matter

1

What I shall learn

- Postulates of the kinetic molecular theory of matter
- Changes in states of matter
- Law of conservation of mass

Introduction

We know that matter is any substance that has mass and occupies space. A piece of bread, a book, aerated soft drinks, the air, steam, etc. all possess mass and occupy space, and are thus known as matter. It is evident from the examples we considered here that matter can exist in three different states, that is, solid, liquid and gas. We have learned in previous classes that all matter is made up of very small particles. The particles in a matter are in constant motion and therefore possess energy. This energy is called kinetic energy. Let us learn about this concept in detail in this chapter.

Kinetic Molecular Theory of Matter

The particles in matter have different amounts of energy, are arranged differently and move in different ways. The kinetic molecular theory of matter explains the properties of different states of matter. The main postulates of the theory are as follows:

1. Matter is made up of minute particles called atoms, ions or molecules that are constantly moving. This energy in motion is called **kinetic energy**.
2. The particles are identical in all aspects.
3. The amount of kinetic energy in a substance varies depending on the temperature. If there is an increase in temperature, the particles of matter gain more kinetic energy and move faster. Particles in the solid state have the least amount of energy, while gas particles have the greatest amount of energy.
4. A change in phase or state occurs when the temperature of the particles in a substance changes sufficiently.
5. All particles in a matter/substance are arranged in a particular or specific manner, which gives its shape to the matter. Also, due to such specific arrangement, there is space between particles. This space is called the **inter-particle space** and it is related to the state of matter of that substance.
6. There are attractive forces in between particles called the **inter-particle attraction**. The strength of these forces increase as the particles get closer to each other.

Table 1.1 Characteristics of the particles in solids, liquids and gases

Characteristic	Solid	Liquid	Gas
Shape	Definite shape	No definite shape. It takes the shape of the container.	No definite shape. It takes the shape of the container.
Volume	Definite volume	Definite volume	No definite volume. It fills the entire volume of the container.
Ability to flow	Cannot flow	Flows from a higher level to a lower level	Flows in all directions
Compressibility	Incompressible	Can be compressed to some extent	Highly compressible
Diffusion	Does not occur	Can occur easily	Can occur quickly
Free surface	Many	One	None
Density	High	Medium	Least
Arrangement of particles	Closely and orderly packed	Closely but randomly packed	Loosely and randomly packed
Inter-particle space	Minimum	More than in solids	More than in solids and liquids
Inter-particle attraction	Strongest	Less than that of solids	Very weak
Movement of particles	Restricted movement	Easy movement	Free movement
Diagram	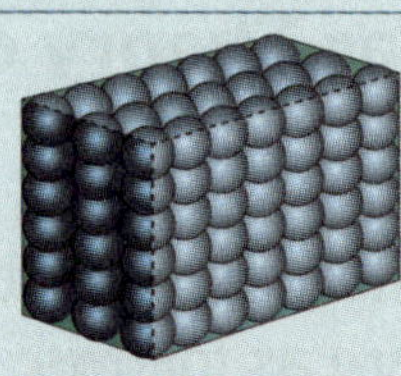	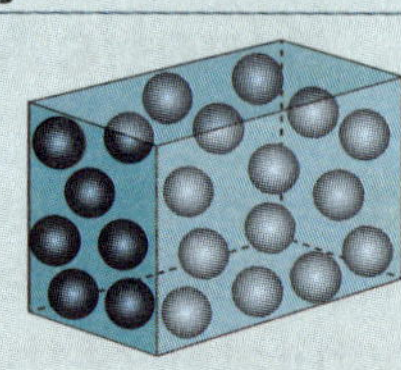	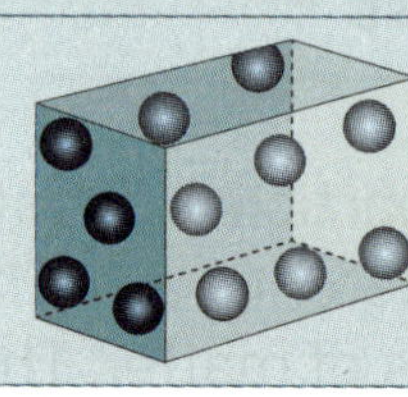

Changes in States of Matter

A matter can change its state depending upon conditions like pressure and temperature. For example, water at 0°C exists as ice (solid). When heated, ice melts into water (liquid) and upon continuous heating, water gets converted into steam (gas).

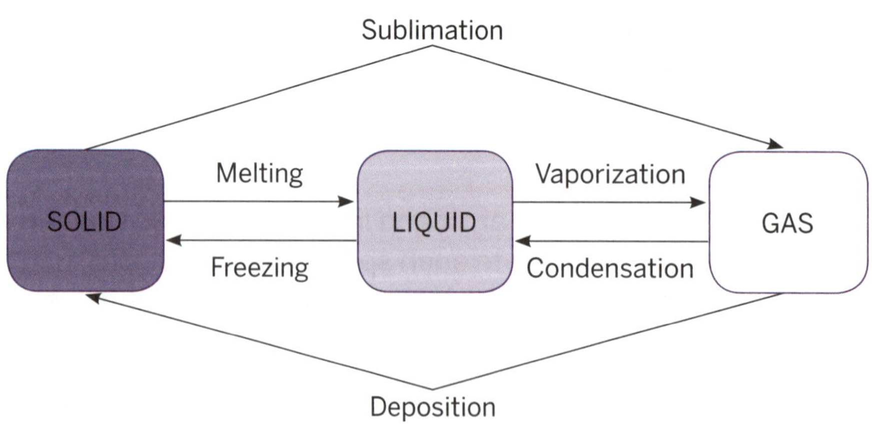

▲ Interconversions of the three states of matter

Let us discuss some processes in which changes in the states of matter take place.

Melting

The conversion of a substance from its solid state to its liquid state at a particular temperature and constant pressure is called **melting/fusion**. Particles in a solid tend to move faster when they are subjected to heat. This increases the kinetic energy of the particles and the same can be recorded on a thermometer as temperature. At a certain point, the speed of the particles is maximum and this corresponds to the maximum temperature which is called the **melting point** of the solid. On further heating, the particles in the solid move apart without any change in their kinetic energy. This movement increases the inter-particle space between the particles. The temperature remains the same until the solid is converted into its liquid state.

Freezing

The conversion of a substance from its liquid state to its solid state at a particular temperature and constant pressure is called **freezing/solidification**. Particles in a liquid possess some kinetic energy and the same can be recorded on a thermometer as temperature. When a liquid is cooled, the speed of its particles slows down, with a direct proportional decrease in its temperature. At a certain point, the speed of the particles is minimum and this corresponds to the minimum temperature which is called the **freezing point** of the liquid. On further cooling, the particles in the liquid move closer together without any change in their kinetic energy. This movement decreases the inter-particle space between the particles. The temperature remains the same until the liquid is converted into its solid state.

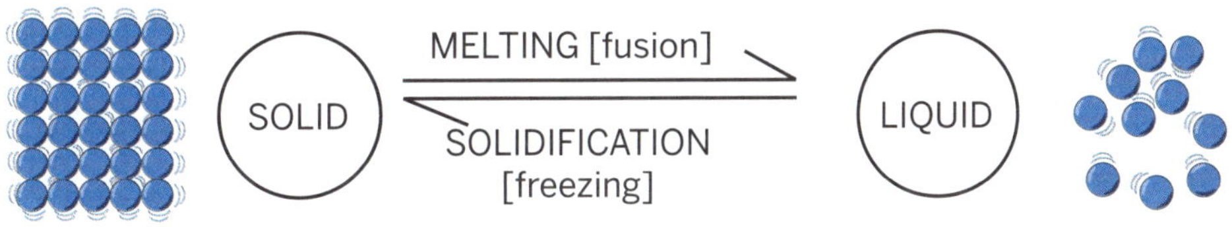

▲ Melting and freezing of matter

Boiling and Vaporization

The conversion of a substance from its liquid state to its gaseous state is called **vaporization**. When this conversion happens at a particular temperature and constant pressure, it is called **boiling**. Particles in a liquid possess some kinetic energy and the same can be recorded on a thermometer as temperature. When a liquid is heated, its particles begin to move faster, with a direct proportional increase in its temperature. At a certain point, the speed of the particles is maximum and this corresponds to the maximum temperature which is called the **boiling point** of the liquid. On further heating, the particles in the liquid move farther apart without any change in their kinetic energy. This movement increases the inter-particle space between the particles. The temperature remains the same until the liquid is converted into its gaseous state.

In vaporization, only the surface particles absorb the heat energy from the surroundings, thus increasing the kinetic energy of the particles in a liquid. When the kinetic energy is sufficiently large, the particles from their liquid state break free and vaporize.

Condensation

The conversion of a substance from its gaseous state to its liquid state at a particular temperature and constant pressure is called **condensation**. Particles in a gas tend to move slower when they are cooled. This decreases the kinetic energy of the particles and the same can be recorded on a thermometer as temperature. At a certain point, the speed of the particles is minimum and this corresponds to the minimum temperature which is called the **condensation point** of the gas. On further cooling, the particles in the gas move closer without any change in their kinetic energy. This movement decreases the inter-particle space between the particles. The temperature remains the same until the gas is converted into its liquid state.

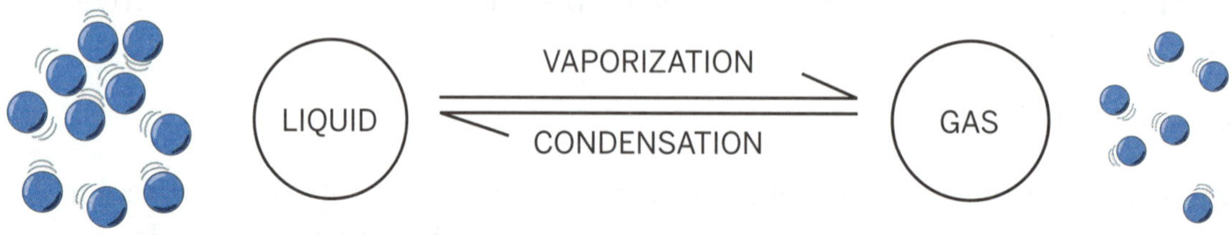

▲ Vaporization and condensation of matter

Sublimation

The conversion of a substance from its solid state to its gaseous state without going through the intermediate liquid state at a particular temperature and constant pressure is called **sublimation**. Particles in a solid possess some kinetic energy and the same can be recorded on a thermometer as temperature. When a solid is heated, its particles tend to move faster, with a direct proportional increase in its temperature. At a certain point, the speed of the particles is maximum and this corresponds to the maximum temperature which is called the **sublimation point** of the solid. On further heating, the particles in the solid move farther apart without any change in their kinetic energy. This movement increases the inter-particle space between the particles. The temperature remains the same until the solid is converted into gaseous state.

▲ Sublimation of matter

Law of Conservation of Mass

The law of conservation of mass states that mass in an isolated system is neither created nor destroyed by chemical reactions or physical transformations.

In other words, in any chemical reaction, the total mass of the reacting substances is equal to the total mass of the products formed, provided masses are measured under similar conditions.

For example, if A and B react to form C and D, then according to the law of conservation of mass,

$$\text{Mass of A} + \text{Mass of B} = \text{Mass of C} + \text{Mass of D}$$

i.e., the total mass of the reactants would be equal to the total mass of the products formed in the reaction. Consider the reaction of sodium chloride (NaCl) and silver nitrate ($AgNO_3$) which results in the formation of silver chloride (AgCl) and sodium nitrate ($NaNO_3$). The mass of each element is written below in the chemical equation for this reaction. We can see that the total mass on both sides of the equation comes out to be equal.

$$NaCl + AgNO_3 \rightarrow AgCl(\downarrow) + NaNO_3$$

$$(23 + 33.5) + (108 + 14 + 48) = (108 + 33.5) + (23 + 14 + 48)$$

$$226.5 = 226.5$$

Activity 1

Aim: To show that mass is neither gained nor lost in a chemical reaction

Materials required: Two beakers, measuring cylinder, chemical balance, chemicals – barium chloride solution and sodium sulphate solution

Procedure:

1. Measure approximately 5 cm^3 of barium chloride solution in the measuring cylinder and pour into one beaker.
2. Rinse the measuring cylinder.
3. Measure approximately 5 cm^3 of sodium sulphate solution in the measuring cylinder and pour into another beaker.
4. Zero the balance and then place both the beakers on the balance at the same time.
5. Accurately measure their total mass and take them off the balance.
6. Carefully pour the contents of one beaker into the other ensuring that it does not spill.
7. Zero the balance again; place both the beakers back on the pan and measure the mass.

(**Note:** Perform the experiment with the assistance of a teacher. Wear an apron and a protection glass. Wash the hands thoroughly after the experiment.)

Observation: On mixing barium chloride with sodium sulphate, a white precipitate of barium sulphate is formed.

$$BaCl_2 + Na_2SO_4 \rightarrow BaSO_4 + 2NaCl$$

$$\text{Barium chloride} + \text{Sodium sulphate} \rightarrow \underset{\text{(White precipitate)}}{\text{Barium sulphate}} + \text{Sodium chloride}$$

Conclusion: On measuring using the chemical balance, we find that the mass of the products (barium sulphate and sodium chloride) formed is equal to the mass of the reactants (barium chloride and sodium sulphate).

Revision Zone

Write T for True and F for False.

1. In a solid, diffusion takes place very slowly.
2. In a gas, the particles are closely packed.
3. Gaseous substances are compressible unlike the solid substances.
4. The process of gases converting into liquids upon cooling is called condensation.
5. Sublimation is the process in which a liquid, on being heated, converts into its solid state.

Keywords

Kinetic energy: energy which a particle possesses by virtue of its movement

Inter-particle space: empty spaces between the particles in a matter

Inter-particle attraction: the attractive force between the particles in a matter

Melting: the process of conversion of a solid into liquid upon heating

Freezing: the process of conversion of a liquid into solid upon cooling

Boiling: the process of conversion of a liquid into gas when subjected to heat externally

Vaporization: the process of conversion of a liquid into gas by the absorption of heat from the surroundings

Condensation: the process of conversion of a gas into liquid upon cooling

Sublimation: the process of conversion of a solid into gas without the formation of the intermediate state

In a Nutshell

- Matter exists in three different states: solid, liquid and gas.
- All matter is made up of minute particles.
- The particles of matter have particular arrangements in their respective states.
- All particles are in constant motion and hence possess kinetic energy.
- Movement of particles increases or decreases with the change in temperature and pressure.
- According to the law of conservation of mass, in a chemical reaction, the total mass of the reactants is equal to the total mass of the products formed.

Exercise

1 Choose the correct answer for each of the following.

a. Which of the following has a definite volume and a definite shape?

i. Chair ii. Apple juice

iii. Oil iv. Shampoo

b. Gases occupy all the available space because their particles are

i. strong

ii. weak

iii. very loosely packed

iv. tightly packed

c. The process in which a liquid converts into solid upon cooling is called

i. vaporization ii. condensation

iii. melting iv. freezing

d. The boiling point of a substance is the temperature at which a substance changes from

i. a liquid to solid

ii. a solid to liquid

iii. a liquid to gas

iv. a gas to solid

e. The law of conservation of mass states that mass cannot be

i. Changed or created

ii. Burnt or destroyed

iii. Dissolved or disposed

iv. Created or destroyed

2 Fill in the blanks.

a. Solidification is also termed as ________. (fusion/freezing)

b. The ________ (potential / kinetic) energy of particles in a solid is very low.

c. The force of ________ (attraction/ repulsion) of particles of matter in gases is negligible.

d. The inter-particle ________ (space/ force) is the maximum between the particles of gases.

e. Inter-particle space between the particles of a solid is ________. (minimum/maximum)

3 Write T for True and F for False.

a. On heating a solid at its melting point the inter-particle space increases.

b. On heating a sublimable solid, the inter-particle attraction is lost.

c. The inter-particle attraction between the particles of gases is maximum.

d. A substance changes from its liquid state to gaseous state at its melting point.

e. Atoms are the only minute particles that constitute the formation of matter.

4 Name the following.

a. The constant temperature at which a liquid changes to solid is ________.

b. The force of attraction between the particles in matter is ________.

c. The process in which a liquid is converted into gas is ________.

d. The process in which a solid changes its state to gas is ________.

e. The temperature at which a liquid is formed from solid is ________.

5 Define the following terms.

a. Melting

b. Freezing

c. Vaporization

d. Boiling

e. Condensation

f. Sublimation

g. Kinetic energy

6 Answer the following questions in brief.

a. State the kinetic molecular theory of matter.

b. State the law of conservation of mass.

c. What is the difference between vaporization and boiling?

d. What is sublimation? Explain.

e. How are melting point and boiling point of a substance different from each other?

7 Answer the following questions in detail.

a. Write the postulates of the kinetic theory of matter.

b. Explain the law of conservation of mass with the help of an experiment.

c. Write a short note on the inter-particle changes that occur between the solid state and liquid state.

d. What are the characteristics of matter in the liquid state?

e. Explain briefly the changes in states of matter.

8 Think and answer.

If salt is added to ice, it starts melting though the temperature of the mixture lowers to -20°C from 0°C. Explain why?

9 Project

Prepare a chart showing three different states of matter (solid, liquid and gas) and explain the changes in states of matter with the example of water cycle.

10 In the Library

Find out whether the change in the pressure of a reaction and the presence of impurities affect the temperature with its changes in state of matter.

Worksheet

Subject Integration

a. Does the movement of particles in solids remain the same when they are subjected to heat? If not, why?

____

____

____

b. Does heating have any impact on the kinetic energy of the particles in solids? If so, how?

____

____

____

c. Depict the inter-particle space between the particles of the states of matter formed when solids (e.g., ice cubes) are subjected to continuous heating during the melting process.

Ice cube

Melting →

d. Draw the arrangement of the particles of the state of matter formed during the sublimation process.

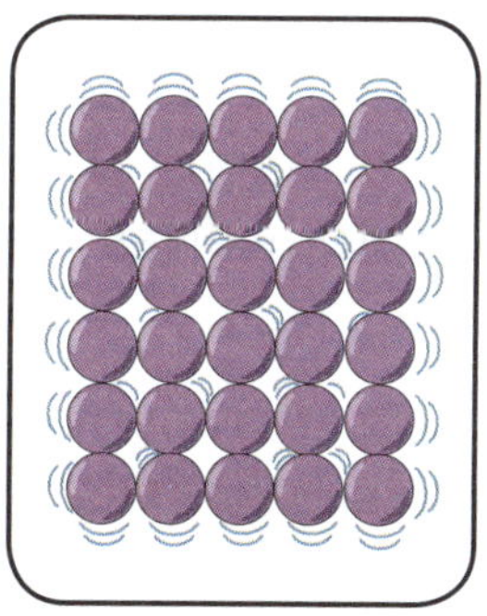

Sublimation →

Physical and Chemical Changes

2

What I shall **learn**

- Types of changes
- Physical changes
- Chemical changes

Introduction

We all must have noticed that changes happen everywhere and at all times around us. For example, melting of ice, rotting of vegetables, dissolving of salt or sugar in water, ripening of fruits, rusting of iron, withering of leaves and flowers, changing of seasons, and growing of seedlings into plants. All these changes involve a change in the properties of the substances. As a result, substances show a change in their size, shape, state, position, colour, composition, etc. Thus, a change can be defined as the conversion of any substance from one form to another.

We have already learned about different types of changes in class 7. In this chapter, we will revise and learn more about the different types of changes.

Types of Changes

Changes can be classified into the following types.

- Natural and artificial changes
- Reversible and irreversible changes
- Exothermic and endothermic changes
- Physical and chemical changes
- Fast and slow changes
- Periodic and non-periodic changes
- Desirable and undesirable changes

Natural and Artificial Changes

▲ Growth of a plant (natural change)

Changes that occur in nature are known as **natural changes**. Examples of natural changes are growth of a plant or a baby, ripening of a fruit, change in seasons, change of day into night, rotation and revolution of Earth, formation of fossil fuels, and occurrence of eclipses and natural disasters (like earthquake, storms and floods).

Changes that are made to happen or caused by human activities are known as **artificial changes**. Examples of artificial changes are making of a pot from clay, a dress from fibres and furniture from wood, cooking of food, construction of dams and bridges, and cutting down of trees to set up factories and cities (leading to pollution and global warming).

▲ Making of a dress from fibres (artificial change)

Fast and Slow Changes

▲ Burning of paper (fast change)

Changes that take place in a very short period of time are known as **fast changes**. These changes occur spontaneously and the products are obtained almost immediately. Examples of fast changes are burning of matchsticks, paper turning into ash when burnt, occurrence of landslides, breaking of glass mirrors, bursting of firecrackers and lightning during a thunderstorm.

Changes that take place over a long period of time are known as **slow changes**. These changes may take hours, days, weeks, months or years to occur. Examples of slow changes are growth of a baby into an adult, formation of fossil fuels, germination of seeds, rusting of iron, growth of fingernails and decay of dead plants.

Greenathon

Collect the seeds of the fruits you eat. Wash the seeds and store them. Whenever you go on a trip, plant these seeds in any barren land that you see. This will help in the growth of new trees.

▲ Germination of seeds (slow change)

Reversible and Irreversible Changes

Changes that can be reversed, that is, we can get back the original substance by changing the conditions that brought about the change, are known as **reversible changes**. In such changes, there might be a change in the look and feel of the substance, but no new substance is formed during or after the change. Thus, the properties of the substance do not change and the change is temporary. Examples of reversible changes are melting of ice, stretching of a rubber band, folding and unfolding of paper, blowing of air into a balloon, boiling of water and dissolving of salt or sugar in water.

▲ Melting of ice (reversible change)

Changes that cannot be reversed, that is, we cannot get back the original substance by changing the conditions that brought about the change, are known as **irreversible changes**. Such changes form new substances after the change. Thus, the properties of the substance change and the change is permanent. Examples of irreversible changes are growth of living things, cooking of rice, ripening of fruits, burning of wood, digestion of food and withering of leaves.

▲ Growth of a baby into an adult (irreversible change)

Periodic and Non-periodic Changes

Changes that repeat after a fixed interval of time are known as **periodic changes**. Examples of periodic changes are change in seasons, phases of the moon, cycle of day and night, rotation and revolution of Earth, movements of the hands of a clock and our heartbeat.

Changes that do not repeat after a fixed interval of time and can occur any time are known as **non-periodic changes**. Examples of non-periodic changes are occurrence of cyclones, earthquakes, tsunamis, volcanic eruptions, accidents and rain showers, and sneezing.

Science in Context

Comets are also differentiated into periodic and non-periodic based on their occurrences.

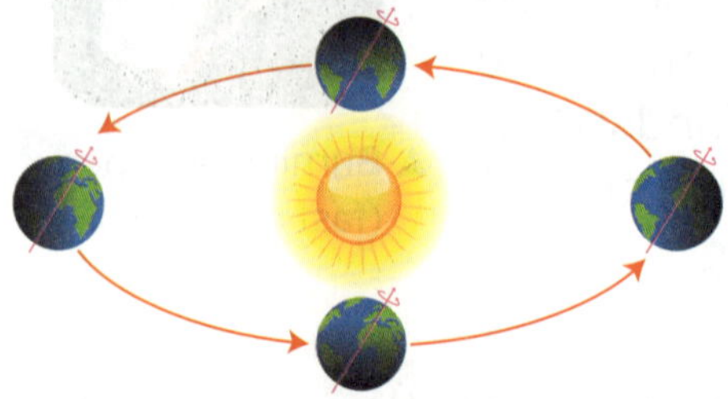

▲ Revolution of Earth (periodic change)

▲ Volcanic eruption (non-periodic change)

Challenge Yourself

Is sweating an exothermic or endothermic change? Give reasons for your answer.

Exothermic and Endothermic Changes

Changes in which there is release of energy in the form of heat are known as **exothermic changes**. Examples of exothermic changes are burning of fuels, bursting of crackers, condensation of water vapour and freezing of water to form ice cubes.

Changes in which there is absorption of energy in the form of heat are known as **endothermic changes**. Examples of endothermic changes are photosynthesis in green plants, cooking of food, evaporation of water and melting of ice cubes.

Do You Know?

When you apply nail polish remover, you feel a cooling effect on your fingers and toes. This is because the acetone present in the nail polish remover absorbs heat from your body while evaporating.

▲ Bursting of crackers (exothermic change)

▲ Photosynthesis (endothermic change)

▲ Cooking of food (desirable change)

Desirable and Undesirable Changes

Changes that are useful to us are known as **desirable changes**. Examples of desirable changes are fermentation of grape juice into wine, formation of curd from milk, cooking of food, ripening of fruits and blooming of flowers.

Changes that are harmful to us are known as **undesirable changes**. Examples of undesirable changes are spoilage of food, occurrence of earthquakes, storms and floods, rotting of fruits and vegetables, soil erosion and rusting of iron.

▲Flood (undesirable change)

A change can be desirable at one time or undesirable at another time based on the situation in which it occurs. A few examples are given below:

- Rain is desirable as it fills up seas, rivers and lakes, but if the same rain occurs in excess and causes floods, it results in loss of both property and life.
- Cutting down of trees for industrialization is desirable as it provides employment to many people, but at the same time, forests are lost which leads to rise in carbon dioxide levels and thus global warming.
- Burning of fossil fuels releases energy that is used in many ways. But along with energy, poisonous gases like carbon monoxide and sulphur dioxide are released that lead to air pollution, which is undesirable.

Find Out

Classify the following into desirable and undesirable changes: formation of curd, tsunami, growth of a plant and breaking of a glass vase.

Revision Zone

Write T for True and F for False.

1. Growth of fingernails is an example of a fast change.
2. Changes that occur in nature are called natural changes.
3. Irreversible change is a temporary change.
4. Soil erosion is a desirable change.

Physical and Chemical Changes

Before we learn about physical and chemical changes, let us first understand what do we mean by physical and chemical properties.

Properties that do not involve any change in the chemical nature of matter are called physical properties. Examples of physical properties include appearance, texture, colour, state of matter, boiling point, melting point, mass, volume, etc. Thus, physical properties can be measured without changing the composition of matter.

Properties that involve a change in the chemical nature of matter are called chemical properties. Examples of chemical properties include pH, heat of combustion, flammability, reactivity with acids, water, metals, etc.

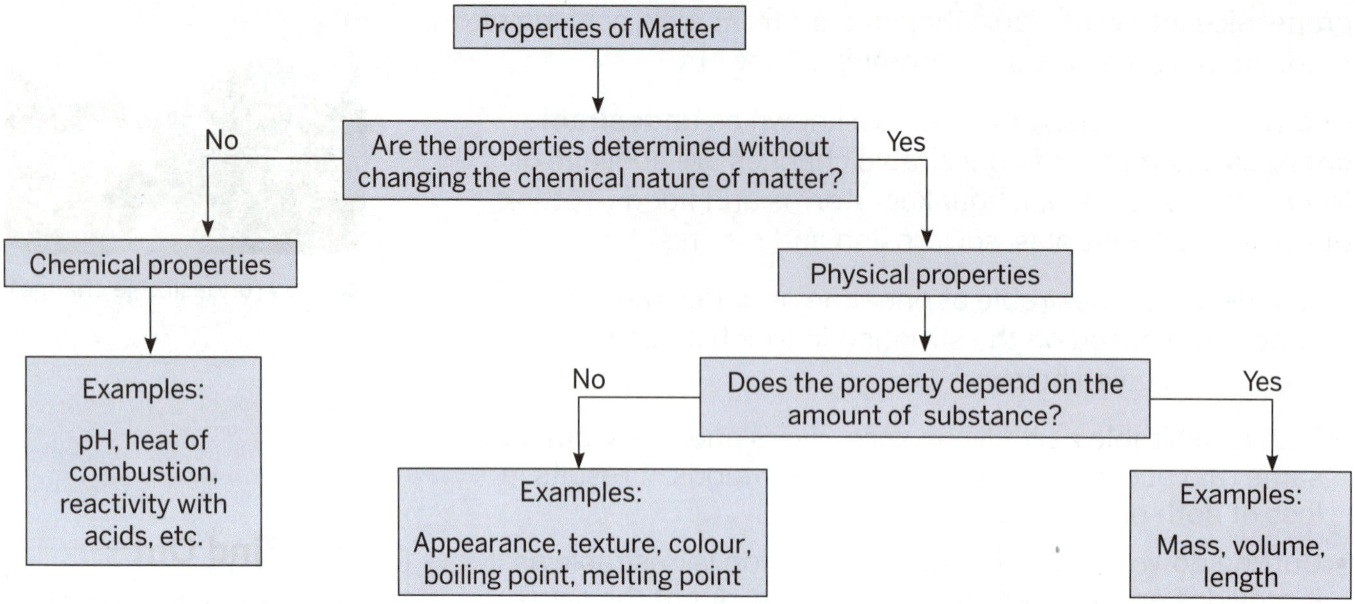

▲ Properties of matter

Physical Changes

Changes in which no new substances are formed are known as physical changes. Such changes might alter the physical properties of the original substance, but the chemical properties remain the same.

Changes in states of matter, that is, processes like boiling, melting, freezing, condensation, sublimation and deposition are all physical changes.

Activity 1

Aim: To prove that evaporation and condensation are physical changes

Materials required: Two beakers, Bunsen burner, water, tripod stand, wire gauze, matchbox, laboratory stand and a lid

Procedure:

1. Take a beaker containing water.
2. Place the beaker on the Bunsen burner and start heating the water.
3. Set up the apparatus as in the figure given alongside.

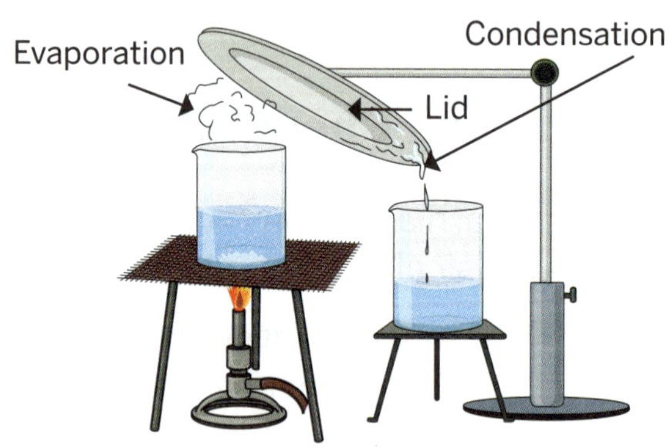

Observation: Upon heating, the water gradually converts into water vapour. When the vapour comes in contact with the cool surface of the lid, it condenses and converts back into liquid water.

Conclusion: Both evaporation and condensation processes are physical changes as no new product is formed.

Activity 2

Aim: To identify the type of change

Materials required: Conical flask, water, sugar, Bunsen burner, tripod stand and wire gauze

Procedure: Take 100 ml of water in a conical flask. Add some sugar and stir until the sugar dissolves. Heat the sugar solution using a Bunsen burner till all the water evaporates. What do you observe? Are sugar crystals found in the flask?

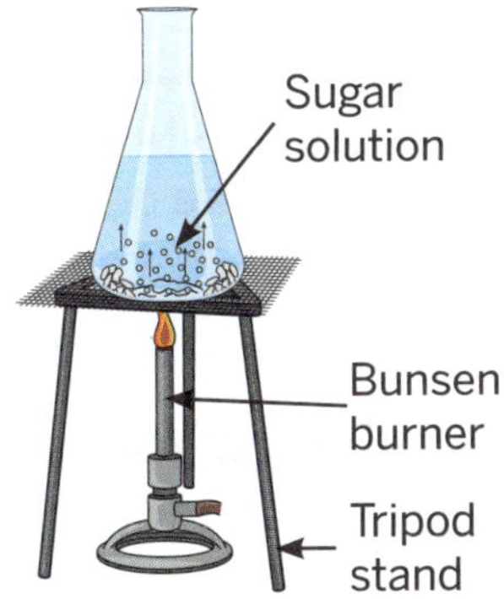

Observation: When the water has evaporated completely, sugar crystals can be seen left at the bottom of the flask.

Conclusion: Dissolving sugar in water is a physical change as there is no formation of any new substance.

From Activity 2, it is clear that dissolution is also a physical change. When sugar is dissolved in water, the sugar molecules only disperse throughout the water. The molecules remain intact and they do not change their chemical identity. The process can be reversed by evaporating water and collecting the sugar crystals. Thus, most of the physical changes are reversible.

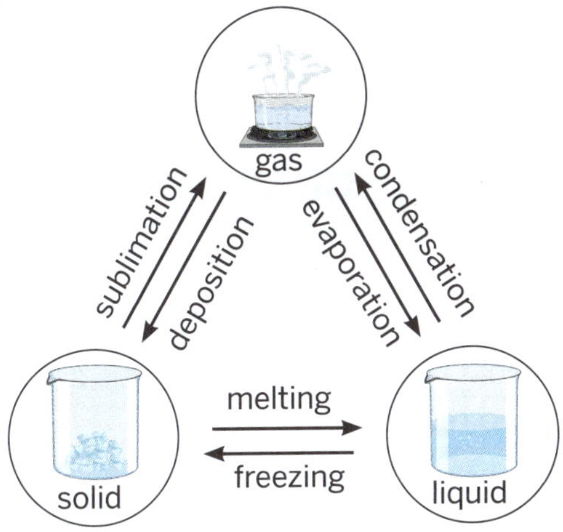

▲ Changes in states of matter

Characteristics of Physical Changes

- No new products are formed.
- There might be a change in the physical properties of the substance, such as shape, size, state, colour and density.
- Chemical properties and composition of the original substance do not change at all.
- Physical changes are mostly temporary and can be reversible or irreversible in nature. For example, melting of ice is a reversible change, whereas breaking of glass is an irreversible change.
- The change in energy is less during physical changes.

Chemical Changes

Changes in which new substances are formed are known as chemical changes. Such changes alter both physical and chemical properties of the original substance. Burning, rusting, explosions, rotting of fruits and vegetables, curdling of milk and formation of curd from milk are a few examples of chemical changes.

▲ Rusting of iron

In the process of rusting, iron (Fe) reacts with oxygen (O_2) and water (H_2O) to form iron oxide (Fe_2O_3) which is a reddish-brown flaky substance. This reddish-brown deposit is known as rust. The process of rusting can be represented as:

$$4Fe + 3O_2 + 2H_2O \longrightarrow 2Fe_2O_3 + 2H_2O$$

When a paper is burnt, it combines with oxygen to form ash and smoke. It is a chemical change, because new substances are formed.

Challenge Yourself

When you try to light a piece of solid wax it melts, but does not burn. If solid wax does not burn, how does a candle burn?

Characteristics of Chemical Changes

- New products are formed.
- Chemical composition and properties of the original substance change.
- Chemical changes are irreversible and permanent in nature.
- Energy change is more during chemical changes than during physical changes.
- During a chemical change, energy is either absorbed or released.

Table 2.1 Differences between physical and chemical changes

Physical changes	Chemical changes
Only the physical properties of substances are changed.	Both the physical and the chemical properties of substances are changed.
Most of the physical changes are temporary and reversible.	All chemical changes are permanent and irreversible.
No new products are formed.	New products are formed with properties different from the original substances.
The amount of energy absorbed or released is minimal or negligible.	A significant amount of energy is absorbed or released.

Signs of a Chemical Change

Following are a few indicators for a chemical change. If two or more of these signs are observed, mostly it can be a chemical change.

- Change in colour
- Change in odour
- Change in temperature
- Production of heat and light
- Production of gas
- Formation of precipitate

Change in colour: Some changes show a change in the colour of the reactants, that is, the colour of the product may differ from that of the reactants. For example, when an acid is added to red cabbage indicator, it changes its colour from purple to pink. And when a base is added to the indicator, it changes into blue colour.

Change in odour: In some changes, when two or more substances are mixed, a distinct odour is produced. Then it is a result of a chemical change.

Change in temperature: When carbon dioxide is bubbled through calcium hydroxide solution, a considerable amount of heat is produced during the reaction. The heat produced warms up the water.

$$Ca(OH)_2 + CO_2 \longrightarrow CaCO_3 + H_2O + \text{Heat}$$

Production of heat and light: When a hydrocarbon reacts with oxygen to form carbon dioxide and water vapour, a lot of heat and light is released. This type of chemical reaction is called combustion reaction.

$$CH_4 + 2O_2 \longrightarrow CO_2 + 2H_2O + \text{(light and heat)}$$

Production of gas: When dilute hydrochloric acid is added to a test tube containing granulated zinc, hydrogen gas is evolved.

$$Zn + 2HCl \longrightarrow ZnCl_2 + H_2 + \text{Heat}$$

Formation of precipitate: When a solution of silver nitrate is added to the solution of sodium chloride, a white precipitate of silver chloride is formed.

$$AgNO_3 + NaCl \longrightarrow \underset{\text{(precipitate)}}{AgCl} + NaNO_3$$

A precipitate is an insoluble solid that forms during a chemical reaction and separates out as a different mass or layer in the solution.

Physical Changes that Show Signs of Chemical Changes

Some changes can be easily classified as a physical change or a chemical change. For example, melting of ice is a physical change, while boiling of an egg is a chemical change. But some changes are not easy to classify. The evidences for a chemical change are change in colour, change in temperature, production of gas and formation of precipitate. But sometimes, these indications may be the result of a physical change.

The following are examples of physical changes where signs of chemical changes are observed.

(a) **Change in colour:** Dissolving food colouring in water results in a colour change. This colour change is caused due to the dissolution of the colouring agents. Moreover, no new products are formed, and hence, this is a physical change and not a chemical change.

(b) **Change in temperature:** When water is heated, there will be a change in temperature. However, as the chemical property of water is not affected due to heating, this is a physical change and not a chemical change.

(c) **Production of gas:** When a carbonated drink is poured into a glass, bubbles of carbon dioxide gas rise to the surface. This could be misunderstood for a chemical change but the formation of bubbles is only a physical phenomenon in this case.

▲ Formation of bubbles in carbonated drinks

▲ A burning candle

Burning of a Candle

When a candle burns, both physical and chemical changes occur. The melting of the solid wax to form liquid wax and the evaporation of liquid wax to form wax vapour are physical changes. When this wax vapour combines with atmospheric oxygen, it gives heat and light and during this process, carbon dioxide is released. Thus, in few cases, both physical and chemical changes take place at the same time.

Revision Zone

Classify the following changes as physical or chemical.

1. Beating aluminium to make foil
2. Sublimation of camphor
3. Formation of water vapour
4. Making pickle from amla
5. Heating of an iron rod to soften it

Keywords

Change: the conversion of any substance from one form to another

Periodic changes: changes that repeat after a fixed time interval

Non-periodic changes: changes that occur any time and do not repeat after a fixed time interval

Physical changes: changes in which no new substances are formed

Chemical changes: changes in which new substances with different properties are formed

Precipitate: Insoluble solid that forms during a chemical reaction and separates out as a different mass or layer in the solution

In a Nutshell

- Change is the conversion of any substance from one form to another.
- Changes are classified into different types: natural and artificial, fast and slow, reversible and irreversible, periodic and non-periodic, desirable and undesirable, exothermic and endothermic, and physical and chemical.
- Changes in which no new substances are formed are known as physical changes. Some examples are folding of a paper, cutting of an iron rod into pieces and melting of butter.
- Changes in which new substances are formed are known as chemical changes. Some examples are burning of paper, cooking of food and rusting of iron.
- The indications of a chemical change are change in colour, change in temperature, heat or light is given off, production of bubbles or gases and formation of precipitate.

Exercise

1 Choose the correct option for each of the following.

a. Which of the following is a reversible change?
   i. Melting of wax
   ii. Boiling of vegetables
   iii. Baking of biscuits
   iv. Frying of food products

b. Which of the following is a periodic change?
   i. Cyclone   ii. Phases of moon
   iii. Accident   iv. Tsunami

c. Which of these is a physical change?
   i. Rusting of iron
   ii. Burning of paper
   iii. Folding of paper
   iv. Cooking of food

d. Identify the characteristic of a chemical change.
   i. Change in both physical and chemical properties
   ii. No new products are formed
   iii. Temporary and reversible
   iv. Energy change is minimal

e. Which of the following is a chemical property?
   i. Boiling point   ii. Texture
   iii. pH   iv. Mass

f. Which of the following is not an indication of chemical change?
   i. Change in colour
   ii. Change in shape
   iii. Change in temperature
   iv. Change in odour

g. Which of the following statements is correct?
   i. Mostly chemical changes are reversible
   ii. Volume is a chemical property of a substance
   iii. Rusting of iron is an example for physical change
   iv. A precipitate is the insoluble solid that forms during the chemical reaction

2 Fill in the blanks.

a. Cutting down of trees is a/an __________ (natural/artificial) change.
b. Germination of seeds is a __________ (fast/slow) change.
c. __________ (Boiling of water/Baking a cake) is a physical change.
d. All chemical changes are __________ (temporary/permanent) changes.
e. Curdling of milk is a __________ (physical/chemical) change.
f. A precipitate is an __________ (soluble/insoluble) solid that forms during a chemical reaction.

3 Write T for True and F for False.

a. Burning of a matchstick is a fast change.
b. All changes in nature are reversible.
c. In a physical change, physical property of the substance is changed.
d. Evaporation is a physical change.
e. Change in temperature is a feature of a chemical change.
f. During a chemical change, new products are formed.

4 Define the following terms.

a. Desirable changes
b. Exothermic changes
c. Physical properties
d. Chemical properties
e. Rusting

5 Differentiate between the following.

a. Natural and artificial changes
b. Fast and slow changes
c. Reversible and irreversible changes
d. Periodic and non-periodic changes

6 Answer the following questions in brief.

a. Define the term change. Give any two examples of a fast change.
b. What is a physical change? Give examples.
c. What is a chemical change? Give examples.
d. Why do materials rust?
e. Give an example of a physical change that shows signs of a chemical change.
f. Burning of a candle is both a physical and a chemical change. Why?

7 Answer the following questions in detail.

a. Distinguish between exothermic and endothermic changes. Explain with examples.
b. A change can be desirable at one time or undesirable at another time. Justify this statement with examples.
c. List the characteristics of physical and chemical changes.
d. What are the different indicators for a chemical change? Give examples.

8 Think and answer

Most chemical changes in your daily life cannot be reversed. However, under right conditions, certain chemical changes can be reversed. What has to be done to reverse a chemical change? (Hint: Recombination of atoms)

9 Project

Dissolving sugar in water is a physical change. However, dissolving salt in water is considered as a chemical change. Conduct an experiment to prove that dissolving salt is a chemical change.

10 In the Laboratory

Materials required: Steel wool (wire sponge) and vinegar

Procedure:

- Place steel wool in a cup and add 100 ml of vinegar into it.
- Wait for 20 minutes and record your observations.

Did you observe any change? If yes, what is the type of change: physical or chemical? What evidence will you provide to prove it as a physical or a chemical change?

Worksheet

Subject Integration

Few examples of changes are listed in the table given below. Mention the category to which the following changes fall into. Put a tick mark (✓) against the correct answers under the appropriate columns.

Type of change	Slow change	Irreversible change	Desirable change	Undesirable change	Chemical change
Curdling of milk					
Digestion of food					
Photosynthesis					
Fermentation					
Ripening of fruits					
Blooming of flowers					
Rotting of vegetables and fruits					
Spoilage of food					
Cutting down of trees					
Germination of seeds					
Withering of leaves					
Growth of a baby into an adult					
Growth of fingernails					
Decay of dead plants					
Formation of fossil fuels					

Elements, Compounds and Mixtures

3

Introduction

What I shall learn

- Elements
- Compounds
- Mixtures
- Methods of separation of mixtures

We use a variety of substances in our daily life. Each substance around us is made of matter. For example, the food we eat, the water we drink, the air we breathe, non-living objects like table, chair, book, stars and clouds, and living things are all made of **matter**. All the things mentioned above have mass and occupy a certain space. Therefore, matter can be defined as anything that has mass and occupies space.

We have learned that each substance has a unique composition and substances have different properties due to differences in their state, size, weight, etc. Based on their composition, all substances (or matter) in nature can be broadly classified into pure and mixed substances. Mixed substances are also called mixtures or impure substances. Most of the substances found in nature are mixtures. Let us revise the related concepts we have learned in the previous classes.

Pure Substance

A substance that consists of only one kind of atoms or molecules is called a **pure substance**.

There are two types of pure substances: elements and compounds.

Elements

A substance that is made up of only one kind of atoms is called an **element**. Every element has its own unique properties. For example, iron contains only one kind of atoms, that is, iron atoms. Other examples of elements are carbon, sodium, gold and oxygen.

Following are the characteristic features of elements:

- Elements consist of only one kind of atoms.
- Each element has its own unique, individual properties.
- The atoms of an element show the same properties as the element.
- Elements cannot be separated or broken down into simpler components by physical or chemical methods.

How to Represent Elements

Elements or atoms of an element are represented using symbols. The representation of an element using the short form or abbreviation of its name is known as its **chemical symbol**.

Table 3.1 Some elements and their symbols

Element	Symbol	Element	Symbol
Helium	He	Phosphorus	P
Nitrogen	N	Magnesium	Mg
Iodine	I	Manganese	Mn
Aluminium	Al	Argon	Ar
Zinc	Zn	Platinum	Pt

Compounds

A **compound** is a pure substance formed when two or more elements combine together in a fixed ratio. The property of a compound is different from the properties of its constituent elements because the elements lose their individual properties when they combine with other elements. For example, carbon dioxide is made up of one atom of carbon and two atoms of oxygen. The properties of carbon dioxide are very different from that of a carbon atom or an oxygen atom. Carbon is a solid but carbon dioxide is a gas.

Following are the characteristic features of compounds:

- Compounds are formed when two or more atoms of different elements combine together chemically in a fixed ratio.
- The properties of compounds are different from the properties of their constituent elements.
- Compounds exhibit their own physical and chemical properties.
- Compounds can be separated into their individual components by chemical methods.

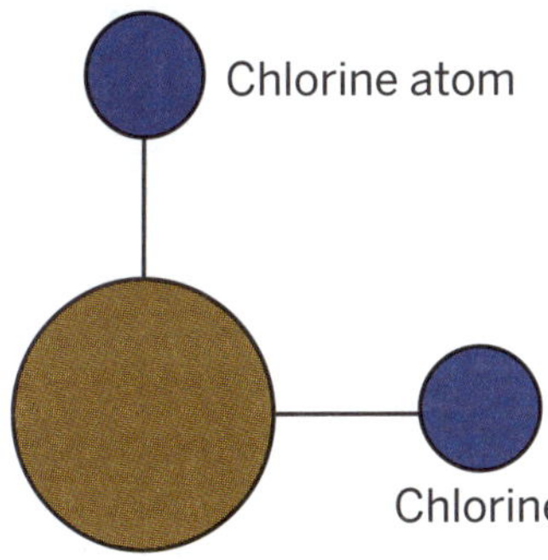

▲ A simple representation of $MgCl_2$

How to Represent Compounds

We know that elements are represented by their symbols. Similarly, the representation of a compound using the symbols of its constituent elements is called its **chemical formula**.

For example, the chemical formula of magnesium chloride is $MgCl_2$. This indicates that it has one atom of magnesium and two atoms of chlorine. Table 3.2 gives the chemical formulae of some compounds.

Remember

When the number of atoms of an element in a molecule is one, then the subscript is not written.

Table 3.2 Some compounds and their formulae

Compound	Formula	Compound	Formula
Water	H_2O	Magnesium oxide	MgO
Sodium chloride (common salt)	NaCl	Copper sulphate	$CuSO_4$
Hydrochloric acid	HCl	Ammonia	NH_3
Sodium carbonate	Na_2CO_3	Methane	CH_4

Significance of a Chemical Formula

A chemical formula gives the characteristics of a compound. The following information can be drawn from a chemical formula:

- The chemical name of the compound
- The elements present in the compound
- The number of atoms of each element present in each molecule of the compound

Mixture

A **mixture** is a substance that contains two or more different substances mixed together in any ratio. Different types of substances present in a mixture are called its components or constituents.

Types of Mixtures

- Based on the state of substances that are mixed together, mixtures can be classified into six types:

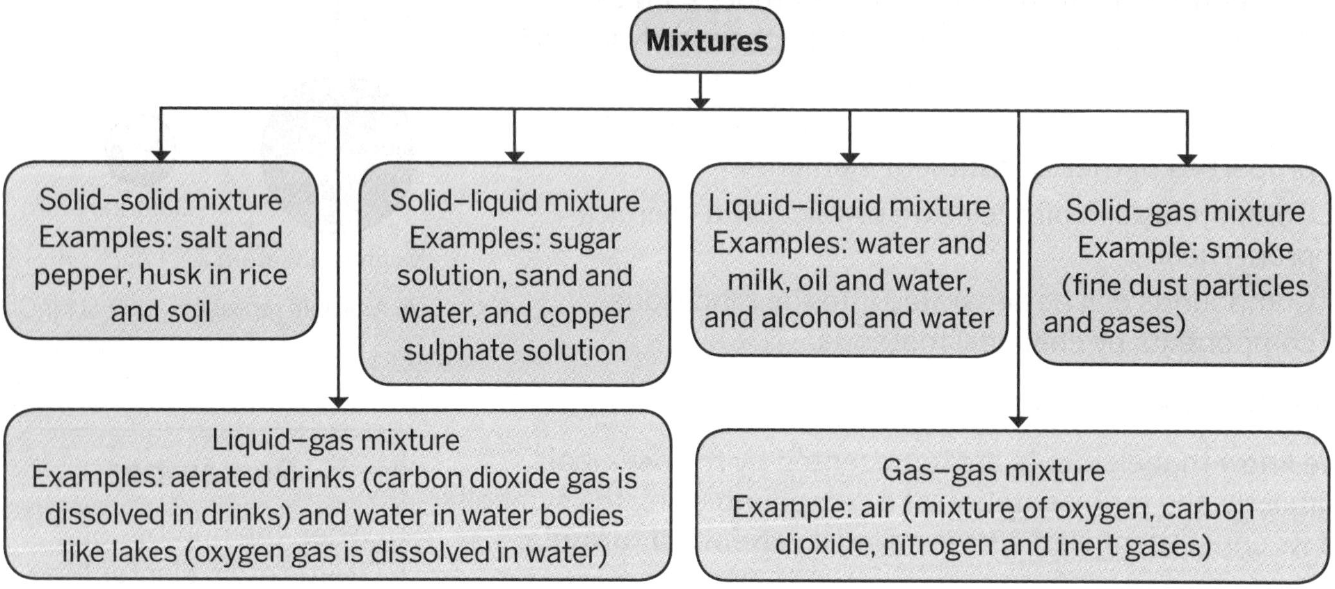

▲ Classification of mixtures

- Based on the extent to which two or more substances can be mixed, mixtures can be classified as homogeneous and heterogeneous.

Homogeneous mixtures: The mixtures in which the components that make up the mixture are distributed uniformly are called **homogeneous mixtures**.

Air is an example of a homogeneous mixture. We cannot see the different gases present in air distinctly. Another example is a mixture of salt dissolved in water.

Heterogeneous mixtures: The mixtures in which the components that make up the mixture are not distributed uniformly are called **heterogeneous mixtures**.

A mixture of oil and water is an example of a heterogeneous mixture. We can see the oil and water distinctly in the mixture.

Separation of Mixtures

We know that a mixture is not a pure substance. It consists of different types of components.

Of these components, some may be useful and some may not be of use. To use only the desirable components, separation is required. Separation of mixtures is necessary due to the following reasons:

- To separate useful components from a mixture. For example, by churning milk, cream is separated from milk so that both the components can be used appropriately.
- To remove unwanted materials or impurities from a mixture. For example, separation of husk from rice grains, unwanted stones from rice grains or pulses before cooking and separation of unwanted leaves from raw leafy vegetables.
- To get desirable or pure substances. For example, in the preparation of tea, tea leaves are separated from brewed tea.

Methods of Separation of Mixtures

Different components of a mixture have different chemical and physical properties. Hence, selecting the appropriate method of separation for a mixture depends on the characteristic properties of each component. Let us look at the various techniques used to separate the components of a mixture.

Separating Solid–Solid Mixtures

1. **Handpicking**: This method of separation is based on differences in size, shape and colour of the two components to be separated. In this method, the component which is lesser in number is picked out using hands.

   Substances that can be separated by handpicking are all types of food grains and pulses having stones, pieces of dirt, husk, etc.

▲ Handpicking

2. **Threshing**: The process of separating grains from stalks of harvested crops either by beating the stalks against a hard surface or by using a threshing machine is called **threshing**.

   Substances that can be separated by threshing are all types of stalks having grains such as wheat, oats, barley, rice, etc.

▲ Threshing

▲ Winnowing

3. **Winnowing**: The process of separating grains (heavier components) from chaff (lighter components) by the action of blowing wind is called **winnowing**.

Substances that can be separated by winnowing are all types of grains which are covered by husk such as rice, wheat, etc.

This method of separation is based on the difference in weight of the two components to be separated.

Activity 1

Aim: To separate a mixture of paper bits and wheat using the winnowing method

Materials required: A mixture of wheat and paper bits, a sheet of cloth, a table fan and a plate or basket

Procedure:

1. Take the mixture in the plate or basket.
2. Spread the sheet of cloth on the floor.
3. Now, stand on a chair or stool and gradually drop the mixture in front of the fan. Observe what happens.

   (Note: The speed of the table fan should be kept at the lowest or medium.)

Observation: Wheat being heavy falls vertically on the sheet of cloth and forms a heap, whereas the paper bits being light get carried away and fall some distance away from the mixture.

4. **Sieving**: The method of using a sieve to separate undesirable components from a mixture is called **sieving**. This method of separation is based on the difference in the sizes of the components to be separated.

▲ Sieving

The larger component which is lesser in number is left behind in the sieve, while the smaller component which is larger in number passes through the pores of the sieve. The desirable component to be separated should have particles whose size is smaller than the sieve pores.

Substances that can be separated by sieving are substances that have bran or impurities in them such as flour, semolina, etc. Wheat flour is sieved before it is used for making dough. During construction of buildings, stones and pebbles are removed from sand by sieving.

Activity 2

Aim: To separate a mixture using the sieving process

Materials required: A mixture of talcum powder, raisins and black pepper, sieves with different pore sizes and a bowl

Procedure:

1. Take the mixture in a sieve with a small pore size.
2. Place a bowl below the sieve and shake the sieve to and fro.
3. Now, take the larger components that were left behind in the sieve.
4. Take a sieve with a pore size larger than that of the previous sieve.
5. Add the components and shake to and fro.
6. Now, much larger components are left behind in the sieve.

Observation: When the mixture is passed through a sieve with a small pore size, the talcum powder separates first, leaving behind black pepper and raisins. Then, when it is passed through a sieve with a larger pore size, the black pepper separates from the mixture, leaving behind only raisins in the sieve. Thus, all the three components of the mixture are separated using the sieving process.

5. **Magnetic separation**: The method of using a magnet to separate magnetic components from a mixture is called **magnetic separation**. This method is based on the difference in the magnetic properties of the components to be separated, that is, a magnetic substance gets attracted to a magnet. In this method, a magnet is rotated over a mixture so that the magnetic components cling to the magnet, while the non-magnetic components are left behind.

   This method is used in industries to remove scrap iron from a garbage heap with the help of a large magnet fitted to a crane.

Activity 3

Aim: To separate a mixture of sand and iron filings using the magnetic separation method

Materials required: Iron filings, sand, bowls and a magnet

Procedure:

1. Make a mixture of sand and iron filings.
2. Place the mixture in a bowl.
3. Now, hover and rotate the magnet over the mixture. What do you see?

Observation: The iron filings get attracted and cling to the magnet leaving behind the sand.

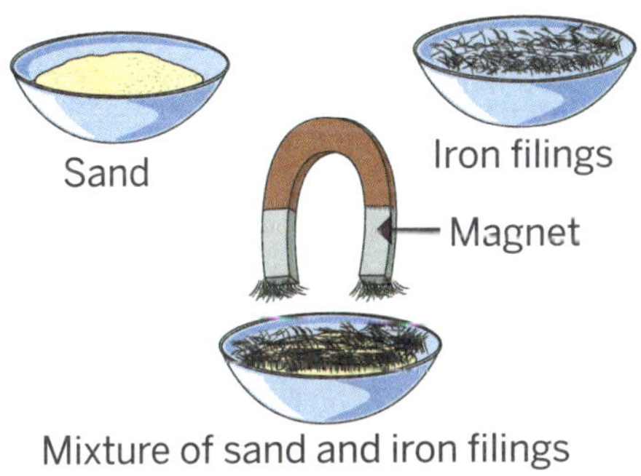

6. **Sublimation**: The process in which a solid changes directly into its gaseous state without passing through its liquid state is called **sublimation**. This method is used when a mixture contains a component that can sublime.

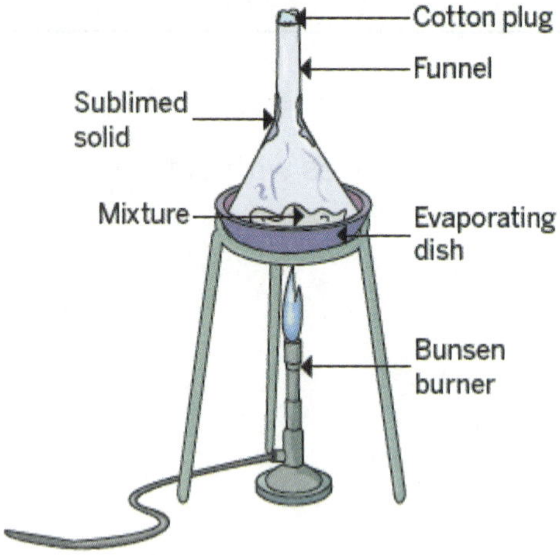

▲ Sublimation

In this method, the mixture is taken in an evaporating dish. When the mixture is heated, the solid component that sublimes evaporates as vapours, leaving behind the component that does not sublime in the dish. Then, the sublimed solid is obtained by cooling the vapours. Thus, the mixture is separated.

Iodine, camphor and ammonium chloride are sublimable substances.

Revision Zone

Fill in the blanks using the correct words.

1. Pebbles and stones can be separated from sand by ________. (sieving/winnowing)
2. The method used by farmers to separate lighter husk particles from heavier seeds of grains is ________. (winnowing/handpicking)
3. Handpicking is a method to separate ________ mixtures. (solid–solid/solid–liquid)
4. The mixture of rice flour and husk can be separated by ________. (threshing/sieving)
5. Stones can be separated from pulses by ________. (handpicking/sieving)

Separating Solid–Liquid Mixtures

To separate solid–liquid mixtures, the selection of the appropriate method depends on whether the solid component is soluble or insoluble in the liquid.

Methods to Separate Insoluble Solids

The following methods are used for separating a solid–liquid mixture when the solid is insoluble in the liquid.

1. **Sedimentation and decantation**: **Sedimentation** is the process of separating insoluble solids mixed in a liquid by allowing them to settle down. Sedimentation takes place due to the difference in the weight of the components of a solid–liquid mixture. So, the heavier solid particles settle down at the bottom of the liquid mixture. The solid particles that settle down during sedimentation are called **sediments**. This method is then followed by decantation in which the heavier insoluble particles that are settled at the bottom are separated by pouring out the top clear liquid into another container without disturbing the sediment.

Thus, the process of pouring out the top clear liquid without disturbing the sediment is called **decantation**.

Sedimentation and decantation processes are used at home while washing pulses with water. The upper layer of water that contains the impurities is decanted and the sediments (pulses) are used further.

Activity 4

Aim: To separate a mixture of sand and water using sedimentation and decantation methods

Materials required: Two beakers, sand, water and a glass rod

Procedure: Take one beaker and fill it half with water. Add a little sand to it. Use the glass rod to mix the contents. Keep the beaker undisturbed for some time. You will notice that the sand particles settle down at the bottom of the beaker. This happens because the sand particles are heavier than water. A clear layer of water will be seen above the settled sand.

Without disturbing the sediment of sand, gently pour out the top layer of water into another beaker. The first beaker will be left with the sediment of sand.

Science in Context

In nature, solid substances such as sand, clay and gravel get transported along with the waves and water currents. These substances get deposited as sediments resulting in the coastline formation. This is the main cause for formation of beaches.

2. **Filtration**: The process of separating insoluble solids suspended in a liquid by using a porous medium (filter) is called **filtration**. Filters with different pore sizes are available. The pores of the filter should be smaller than the size of the components that need to be removed. The insoluble solid component left in the filter is called the **residue**. The liquid that passes through the filter is called the **filtrate**.

▲ Filtration

Activity 5

Aim: To separate a mixture of sand and water using filtration method

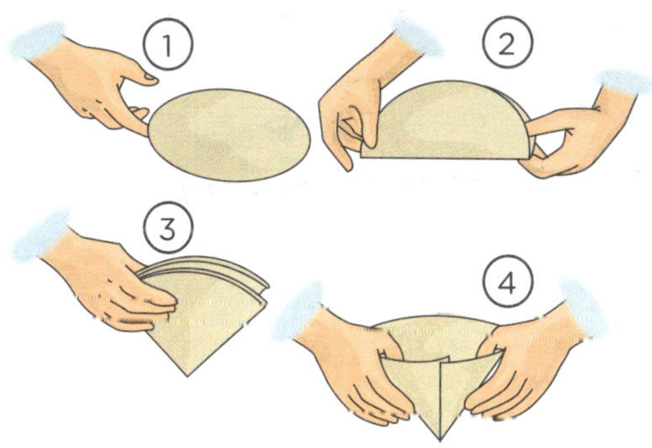

Materials required: Two beakers, sand, water, a glass rod, filter paper and a funnel

Procedure: Take some sand in a beaker. Add some water to it and use the glass rod to mix the contents. Take a filter paper and make a cone as shown in the figure given alongside. Place the paper cone in the funnel and keep an empty beaker below the funnel. Gently pour the mixture into the funnel.

Observation: You will notice that clear water collects in the beaker after passing through the filter paper and sand particles are left behind in the filter paper.

We can use this method of separation at home while making lemon juice or orange juice. The seeds and suspended pulp particles of lemon or orange can be separated from its juice by the filtration method.

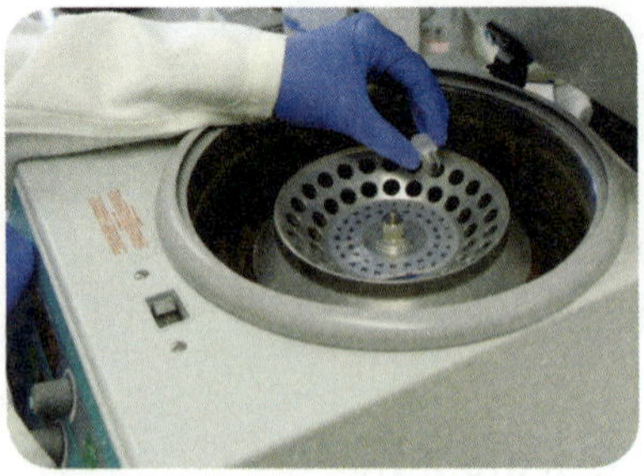

▲ Centrifuge

3. Centrifugation: The process that involves rotating a mixture rapidly in a closed container to separate very fine, insoluble solid components mixed in a liquid is called **centrifugation**.

The machine used for centrifugation is called a **centrifuge**. A centrifuge consists of a rotating motor with holes to place centrifuge tubes. These tubes contain the mixture to be separated. When the centrifuge is switched on, the motor rotates the mixture at a very high speed due to which the heavier components settle down at the bottom of the tubes. The sediment in the tubes is then separated from the liquid by decantation. The lighter components of the mixture remain in the liquid. This method is used in laboratories to separate cells from blood and in dairies to separate cream from milk.

Methods to Separate Soluble Solids

The following methods are used for separating a solid–liquid mixture when the solid is soluble in the liquid.

1. Evaporation: The process in which a liquid converts into its gaseous state is called **evaporation**. This method is used to separate soluble solids from liquids.

▲ Separation of salt from sea water by evaporation

Evaporation is the process used to obtain common salt from sea water. The sea water consists of a large amount of salts in it. The sea water is allowed to flow through narrow channels near coastal areas and get collected in shallow ponds (called salt pans). The water in these salt pans is allowed to evaporate by the heat of the sun. The solid salt is left behind as the water evaporates. The salt is then collected and sent for purification. The purified salt is used for various purposes.

Discuss

What kind of impurities can the salt contain that must be removed before use?

2. Distillation: A separation method used to separate a pure liquid from a mixture or solution by evaporation and then condensation is called **distillation**. The process of distillation is carried out in a special laboratory apparatus. The process involves the following steps:

1. The mixture is heated in a round-bottomed flask. Due to heating, the liquid component in the mixture evaporates to form vapours and the solid component is left behind in the flask.
2. A condenser is fitted to the flask. The vapours of the liquid rise and pass through this condenser where they cool down and condense to form pure liquid.
3. This pure liquid is collected in a separate flask.

Distillation method is used to obtain distilled water, which is considered to be the purest form of water as it does not contain any impurities. Distilled water is used in science laboratories, car batteries and medicines.

Activity 6

Aim: To demonstrate the separation of salt from salt solution using evaporation method

Materials required: China dish, salt solution, wire gauze, Bunsen burner and tripod stand

Procedure:

1. Take some salt solution in a China dish.
2. Heat the solution using a Bunsen burner.
3. Boil the solution until the liquid evaporates completely.

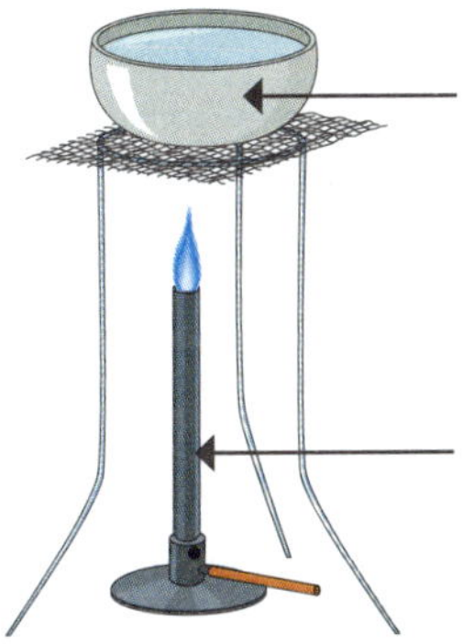

Observation: The solid, white particles of salt are left behind along the inner sides of the China dish after evaporation.

Conclusion: Soluble solids present in a solid–liquid mixture can be separated by evaporation method.

Activity 7

Aim: To demonstrate the separation of solid–liquid mixture using the method of distillation

Materials required: Round-bottomed flask, mixture (solution of salt and water), beaker, condenser, Bunsen burner and laboratory stands

Procedure: The apparatus is set up as shown in the figure.

1. Heat the mixture in the round-bottomed flask.
2. The mixture starts to boil and the liquid component (water) evaporates.
3. The vapours pass through the condenser, where they cool and condense to form the pure liquid that gets collected in the beaker.
4. The solid component (salt) is left behind.

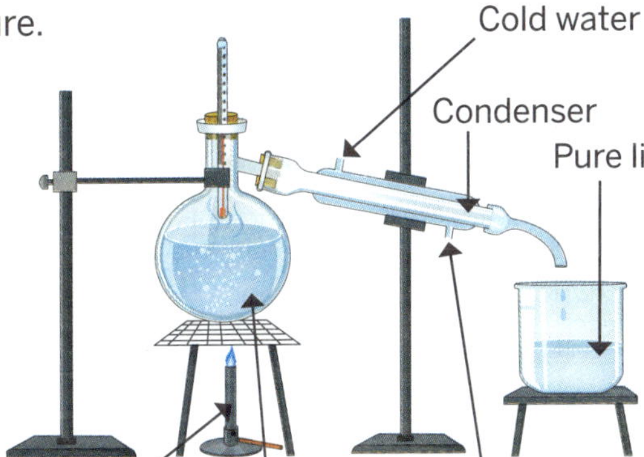

Observation: The liquid component is separated from the solid–liquid mixture leaving behind the solid component. The liquid thus obtained is in its pure form.

Conclusion: Distillation is used to obtain pure liquid from a solid–liquid mixture.

3. Crystallization: The process of separating a solid in the pure form from its solution by forming crystals is known as **crystallization**. Common salt obtained from sea water is purified using the process of crystallization. Common salt (sodium chloride) is obtained from sea water by evaporation. The salt obtained by this process consists of many impurities such as sand, magnesium chloride, etc. Thus, the impure salt is purified through crystallization.

For crystallization, a large amount of salt is dissolved in water. The solution is heated and, if needed, more salt is added to the solution till it becomes a saturated solution. The solution is then filtered to separate the insoluble impurities present in it. The filtrate is then allowed to cool and the salt present in the solution aggregates to form crystals. The salt crystals are separated by filtration and then dried.

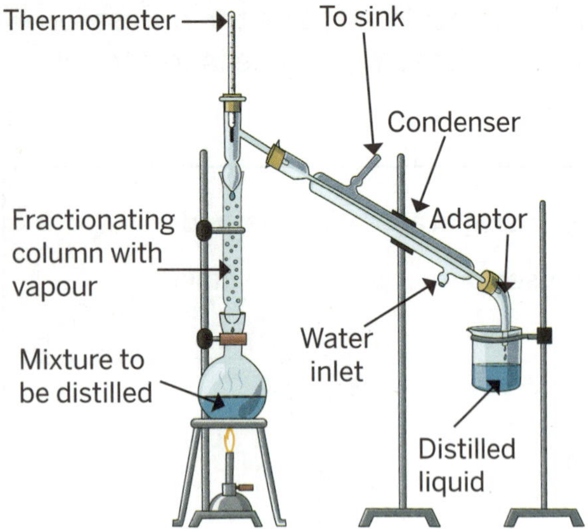

▲ Set-up of fractional distillation

Separating Liquid–Liquid Mixtures

1. Fractional distillation: Fractional distillation is the method used to separate a mixture of miscible liquids (liquids that can be mixed together completely). This method is based on the difference in the boiling points of the liquid components to be separated. The apparatus used for this method consists of a distillation flask, fractionating column, a condenser and heat supply. When a mixture of two liquids is heated in the distillation flask, it boils and vapours rise up to the fractionating column. As the vapours go up in the column, the temperature inside the column begins to decrease. So, in the mixture, the liquid with a lower boiling point vaporizes first, rises to the top of the column and passes through the condenser. Here, the vapours cool down and condense to form a liquid which collects in a container. The vapours of the liquid with a higher boiling point condense and collect at the bottom of the fractionating column itself. Therefore, both the liquids boil at different temperatures and get collected. This method is used to get petroleum products from crude oil, such as petrol, kerosene, diesel, gasoline, petroleum gas and tar.

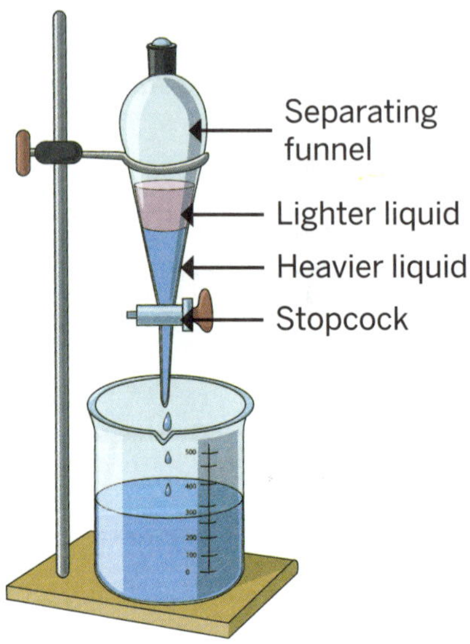

▲ Separation using a separating funnel

2. Separating funnel: A separating funnel is used to separate a mixture of immiscible liquids. This method is based on the principle that in immiscible liquids, the lighter liquid floats above the layer of the heavier liquid.

A separating funnel is a glass apparatus that is narrow at the bottom with a stopcock (like a tap). The funnel has an opening at the top to pour the liquid mixture. After the liquid mixture is poured, it is left undisturbed for some time. Immiscible liquids form separate layers with the heavier liquid at the bottom and the lighter liquid at the top. When the stopcock is opened, the heavier liquid at the bottom moves out first and is collected in a separate container. When the bottom layer flows out completely, the stopcock is closed. Only the lighter liquid remains in the separating funnel. Thus, the two liquids are separated.

A mixture of oil and water can be separated using this technique.

Revision Zone

Write T for True and F for False.

1. Decantation is the best process for removing tea leaves from tea.
2. A mixture of milk and water can be separated by sedimentation and decantation.
3. The preferred method to recover clear water from a bucket of muddy water is filtration.
4. Evaporation is used to obtain salt from sea water.

Keywords

Pure substance: a substance that consists of only one kind of atoms or molecules

Mixture: a substance that contains two or more different substances mixed together in any ratio

Homogeneous mixtures: The mixtures in which the constituents that make up the mixture are distributed uniformly

Heterogeneous mixtures: The mixtures in which the constituents that make up the mixture are not distributed uniformly

Threshing: The process of separation of grains from stalks by beating the stalks against a hard surface or by using threshing machines

Sieving: a method that uses a sieve to separate undesirable components from a solid–solid mixture

Winnowing: a method that uses the action of wind to separate undesirable components from a solid–solid mixture

Sedimentation: The process in which the insoluble, heavier particles of a solution settle down at the bottom of the container

Decantation: The process of transferring clear liquid without disturbing the sediment

Filtration: the process of using a porous medium (filter) to separate fine, insoluble solid components suspended in a liquid

Centrifugation: the process of separation of very fine, insoluble solid components mixed in a liquid using a centrifuge

Distillation: the method of separation of components of a mixture through evaporation and condensation

Fractional distillation: the process of separation of a mixture of miscible liquids based on the difference in their boiling points

In a Nutshell

- All matter in nature can be broadly classified into pure substances and mixtures.
- Pure substances can be of two types: elements and compounds.
- Mixtures can be classified into six types: solid–solid mixture, solid–liquid mixture, liquid–liquid mixture, solid–gas mixture, liquid–gas mixture and gas–gas mixture.
- Based on the distribution of components, mixtures can be classified as homogeneous and heterogeneous mixtures.
- Solid–solid mixtures are separated by techniques like handpicking, sieving, winnowing, magnetic separation and sublimation.
- Solid–liquid mixtures are separated by techniques like sedimentation and decantation, filtration, centrifugation, evaporation, distillation and crystallization.
- Liquid–liquid mixtures are separated by techniques like distillation, fractional distillation and using a separating funnel.

Exercise

1 Choose the correct answer for each of the following.

a. A substance that contains two or more substances mixed together is a ________.
   i. compound ii. mixture
   iii. element iv. molecule

b. Which of the following methods is used to clean rice before cooking?
   i. Handpicking ii. Sieving
   iii. Winnowing iv. Filtration

c. Which of the following properties is used to separate a mixture of two solids by winnowing?
   i. Weight difference
   ii. Size difference
   iii. Colour difference
   iv. All of these

d. The process of pouring out the upper layer of clear liquid without disturbing the sediment is called ________.
   i. sedimentation ii. evaporation
   iii. decantation iv. distillation

e. The component of the mixture retained in the filter during filtration is called ________.
   i. residue ii. filtrate
   iii. sediment iv. effluent

f. Sublimation can be used to separate a mixture of
   i. sand and ammonium chloride
   ii. sand and sugar
   iii. iron filings and salt
   iv. stones and rice

g. Which of the following techniques is used to separate two immiscible liquids?
   i. Centrifugation
   ii. Separating funnel
   iii. Filtration
   iv. Decantation

2 Fill in the blanks.

a. A ________ (compound/mixture) is formed when two or more elements combine together chemically.

b. The mixtures in which the components are distributed uniformly are called ________ (homogeneous/heterogeneous) mixtures.

c. The chemical formula for sodium carbonate is ________ ($NaCO_3$/Na_2CO_3).

d. Filtration is used when the substances to be separated are ________ (soluble/insoluble) in a liquid.

e. While using a separating funnel, the first liquid to be collected in a beaker will be ________ (water/oil).

f. Common salt is purified by ________ (centrifugation/crystallization) method.

3 Write T for True and F for False.

a. Compounds are impure substances.

b. An alloy is a homogeneous mixture.

c. Sieving allows fine flour particles to remain in the sieve while the bigger impurities pass through the sieve.

d. Sedimentation is followed by decantation in the separation of solid–liquid mixtures.

e. A centrifuge is used to separate very fine, insoluble solid components from a solution.

f. The chemical symbol of argon is Ar and that of platinum is Pt.

4 Define the following terms.

a. Element

b. Mixture

c. Winnowing

d. Threshing
e. Filtration
f. Crystallization

5 Choose the odd one out. Give reasons for the choice.

a. Iodine, camphor, sugar, ammonium chloride
b. Winnowing, distillation, handpicking, solvent extraction
c. Sieving, evaporation, filtration, centrifugation
d. Distillation, centrifugation, evaporation, crystallization
e. Sugar solution, coffee, tea, lemon juice

6 Differentiate between the following.

a. Homogeneous mixture and heterogeneous mixture
b. Handpicking and winnowing
c. Sedimentation and decantation
d. Evaporation and crystallization
e. Distillation and fractional distillation

7 Answer the following questions in brief.

a. What is the difference between an element and a compound?
b. What is a heterogeneous mixture? Give one example.
c. What is a heterogeneous mixture? Give one example.
d. How is sieving method used at construction sites?
e. Mention the appropriate methods for the separation of the following mixtures:
    i. A solid–solid mixture in which the components have different sizes
    ii. A mixture that has components with different magnetic properties
    iii. A mixture of liquids with different boiling points
f. Name the methods used to separate a solid–liquid mixture.
g. Why is distilled water the purest form of water? Give its uses.

8 Answer the following questions in detail.

a. Define mixture. Mention the different types of mixtures.
b. What are the different methods used to separate a solid–solid mixture? Explain any two.
c. What is a centrifuge? What kind of mixture is separated using it and how?
d. Explain the method of distillation with the help of a diagram.
e. Describe the process of fractional distillation.
f. Explain how immiscible liquids are separated using a separating funnel.

9 Think and answer.

How will you separate the following mixtures? Name the methods that can be used.

a. Sugar, iron filings and wheat
b. $CaCO_3$ and NaCl
c. Kerosene and water

10 Project

1. Visit a water treatment plant and find out how many methods are used to treat the water before it is let into the taps for use. Write a report on the entire process involved in the cleaning of water.
2. Visit some nearby ponds, lakes or rivers that have dried during summer and try to understand the process of evaporation.

11 In the Library

Iron and iron oxide content in water bodies leads to adverse effects on aquatic animals and human beings. What will happen if these toxic substances are not separated from industrial effluents? Collect more information on the effects and diseases caused.

Worksheet

Answer the following.

a. Evaporation and crystallization are methods used to obtain salt from sea water. How are these two techniques different from each other?

____

____

____

____

____

b. Draw a neat labelled diagram of the apparatus used to separate a mixture of oil and water. Also, name the technique used to separate this mixture.

c. Write the principle behind the following separation techniques.

1. Centrifugation: ______________________________
2. Sieving: ______________________________
3. Winnowing: ______________________________
4. Fractional distillation: ______________________________

Atomic Structure

4

What I shall learn

- Earlier views on atomic structure
- Subatomic particles (electrons, protons and neutrons) and their discoveries
- Discovery of nucleus
- Atomic models
- Modern concept of the atom
- Atomic number and mass number
- Electronic configuration
- Valency and variable valency

Introduction

We have learned in our previous classes that everything in this universe is made up of matter and all matter is made up of tiny particles called atoms. In other words, atoms are the building blocks of matter. Atoms were initially thought to be very small particles that cannot be further divided or split into smaller particles. Since then, many scientists from different generations have dedicated their lives to solve the mystery behind these atoms.

In this chapter, we will learn in detail about the contributions of various scientists who were involved in the study of the atom, its structure, properties and constituents.

Earlier Views on Atomic Structure

Maharshi Kanada was an ancient Indian philosopher and scientist of 600 BC. He postulated that matter consists of very small particles, which he termed as *anu*. He also proposed that an *anu* may consist of subatomic particles, which he termed as *paramanu*, meaning a particle that cannot be further divided or broken down.

Democritus, the great Greek philosopher of 400 BC, stated that matter is made up of tiny particles called atoms and these atoms are invisible and indivisible. The word atom comes from the Greek word *atomos* in which *a* means 'not' and *tomos* means 'to cut'. That is, a particle that cannot be cut or divided anymore. Before Democritus, the concept of atom was originally proposed by the Greek philosopher Leucippus who was the teacher of Democritus. Democritus worked on his teacher's assumptions and put forward his ideas.

Dalton's Atomic Theory

John Dalton, an English chemist, postulated the atomic theory. His theory became the theoretical foundation in the field of chemistry. Some of the postulates of Dalton's atomic theory are as follows:

- Matter is composed of tiny particles called atoms.

Know the Scientist

John Dalton (1766–1844) was the first person to explain the difference between an atom and a molecule. His theory supports the law of conservation of mass, which is accepted even today. It also explains the laws of chemical combination. He is also known for his work on colour blindness, which is also known as Daltonism.

- Atoms are indivisible and cannot be created or destroyed.
- All atoms of an element are identical in all aspects, that is, all atoms of an element have the same mass, size and other properties.
- Atoms of different elements are different in all respects, that is, atoms of an element have different mass, size and other properties from atoms of other elements.
- Atom is the smallest unit of matter that takes part in a chemical reaction.
- Atoms of two or more elements combine together in small whole number ratios to form compounds.
- During a chemical reaction, atoms do not change but only rearrange themselves to form new compounds.

John Dalton's atomic theory was later modified as further discoveries were made in this field. Eventually, by the end of the 19th century, it was discovered that atoms are made up of tinier particles, which are called its **subatomic** or **fundamental particles**. These subatomic particles are called protons, neutrons and electrons.

Let us learn about how these particles were discovered and how these discoveries modified the views on atomic structure.

Discovery of Electrons

Electrons were the first subatomic particles to be discovered. In 1897, British scientist J.J. Thomson discovered the negatively charged particles known as electrons through the cathode ray-discharge tube experiment. He received the Nobel Prize in Physics in the year 1906 for his research on cathode rays.

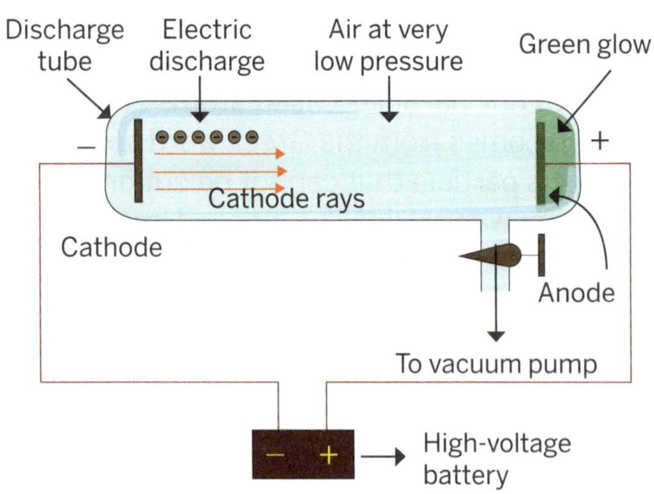

▲ Cathode ray experimental set-up

J.J. Thomson's Cathode Ray Experiment

Thomson used a special tube called discharge tube for his experiment. It is a hard, cylindrical glass tube that consists of two metal plates called electrodes, each sealed at the two ends of the tube. The metal plates are connected to the two terminals of a high-voltage battery.

The metal plate that is connected to the negative terminal acts as a cathode. The metal plate that is connected to the positive terminal acts as an anode. A vacuum pump is connected to one side of the tube to lower the pressure inside the tube.

To perform his experiment, Thomson passed very high-voltage electricity (10,000 volts) through the discharge tube at a very low pressure (nearly 0.001 mm of mercury). The principle behind this experiment was that gases act as poor conductors of electricity under normal conditions, but at a very high voltage and under low pressure conditions, they become good conductors of electricity. His observations during the experiment were as follows:

- A continuous stream of rays was emitted from the cathode and he called these rays as **cathode rays**.
- A fluorescent green glow was observed at the other end of the tube.
- The cathode rays were found to be moving from the cathode region to the anode region.

This proved that these rays consisted of negatively charged particles.

Through his repeated experiments with different gases, he concluded that his observations remained the same.

Characteristics of Cathode Rays

From the various experiments performed by J.J. Thomson, the following characteristics of the cathode rays were found.

- **Cathode rays travel in straight lines**: When an object is placed in the path of cathode rays, a shadow of the object appears at the other end of the discharge tube. This shows that the cathode rays travel in a straight line.
- **Cathode rays consist of fast-moving particles**: If a light paddle wheel is placed in the path through which cathode rays pass, it starts rotating. This proves that the cathode rays consist of a stream of fast-moving particles.
- **Cathode rays are negatively charged**: When an electric field is applied in the path of cathode rays, the rays tend to bend towards the positively charged plate. This proves that cathode rays consist of negatively charged particles and these particles are termed as **electrons**. Thus, it was found that all matter or atoms contain negatively charged particles or electrons.
- **Ratio of electric charge to mass (*e*/*m*) is constant**: Thomson also found out that the charge (e) to mass (m) ratio of the particles that constitute the cathode rays is constant,

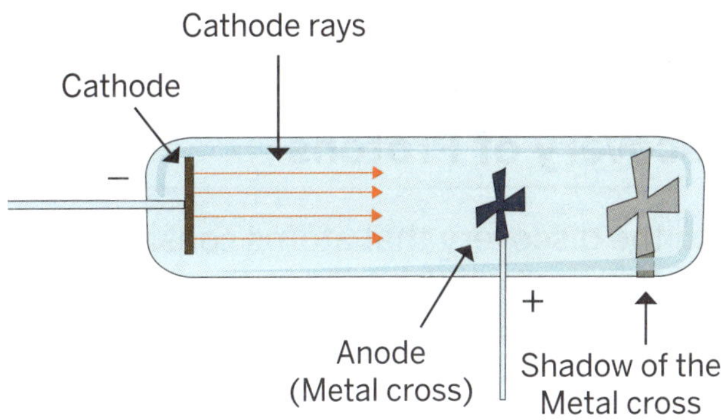

▲ Cathode rays form a shadow if an object is placed in their path

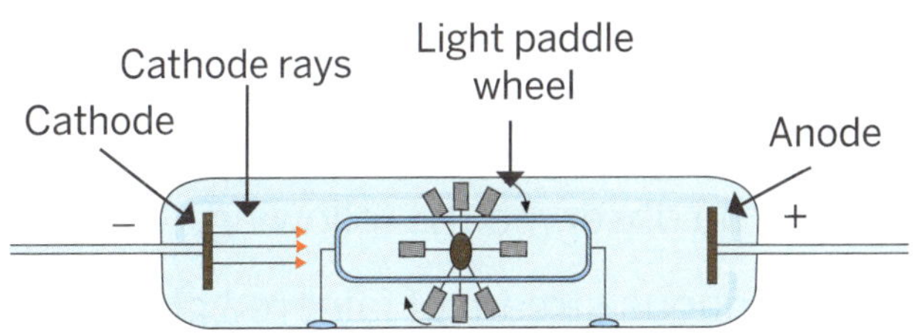

▲ Cathode rays can rotate a paddle wheel if placed in their path

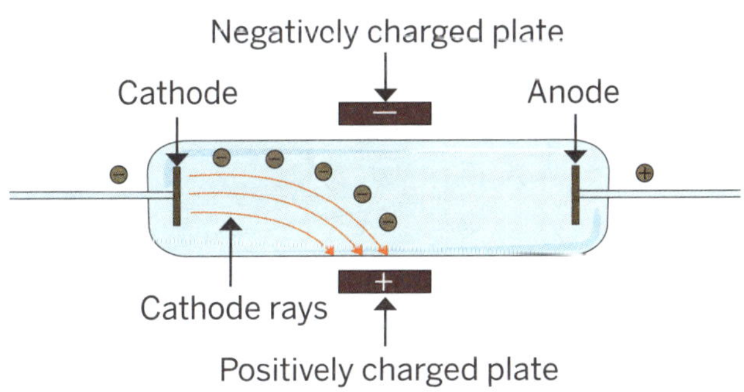

▲ The cathode rays bend towards the positively charged plate

Know the Scientist

Charge of an electron was determined by American experimental physicist **Robert A. Millikan** (1868–1953). He received the Nobel Prize in Physics in the year 1923 for his contribution towards elementary electronic charge and photoelectric effect.

irrespective of the material of the electrodes or the gas used in the discharge tube. The ratio (e/m) was calculated to be 1.78×10^8 coulomb per gram (C/g).

Characteristics of an Electron

- The mass of an electron is 9.1×10^{-31} kg and is equal to 1/1837 times the mass of a hydrogen atom. Mass of an electron is negligible when compared to the mass of an atom.
- Electrons are particles with unit negative charge. One unit charge is given by $e = 1.6 \times 10^{-19}$ coulombs (C). So, the charge of an electron = -1.6×10^{-19} coulombs (C).
- An electron is represented by the symbol ${}_{-1}e^0$, where '0' represents the mass and '–1' represents one unit negative charge.

Discovery of Protons

With the discovery that atoms consist of negatively charged particles called electrons, scientists were of the opinion that atoms must also contain some positively charged particles to neutralize this negative charge of electrons as all atoms are electrically neutral in nature.

In 1886, the German scientist Eugen Goldstein discovered positively charged particles known as protons. He discovered protons while he was working with the cathode ray discharge tube.

Goldstein's Experiment

Instead of a normal cathode in the discharge tube, Goldstein used a perforated cathode (a cathode containing small holes) for his experimental set-up. When high-voltage electricity (10,000 volts) was applied across the terminals at a very low pressure of nearly 0.001 mm of mercury, he observed the following:

- A continuous stream of faint red glowing rays was emitted from the holes in the area at the back of the cathode.

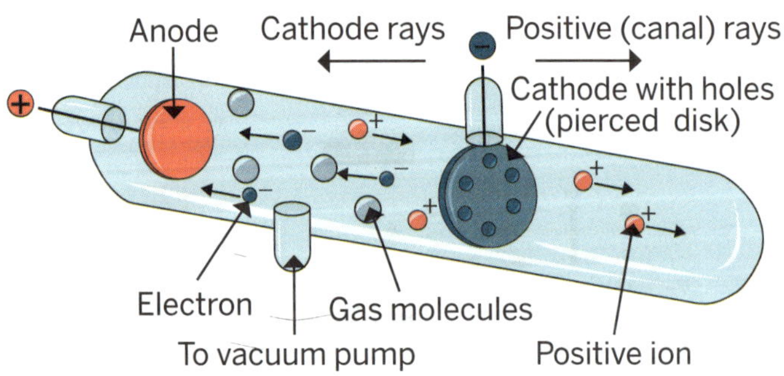

▲ Goldstein's experimental set-up

- These rays were found to be moving in a direction opposite to that of the cathode rays. This proves that these rays consist of positively charged particles.

Goldstein named these rays as **canal rays** or **channel rays**, as they were produced through the holes in the cathode. As these rays were emitted from the anode and were composed of positively charged particles, these rays were also referred to as positive rays or **anode rays**.

Characteristics of Anode Rays

- **Anode rays travel in straight lines**: When an object is placed in the path of anode rays, the shadow of the object appears at the other end of the discharge tube. This shows that anode rays travel in straight lines.
- **Anode rays consist of fast-moving particles**: If a light paddle wheel is placed in the path through which anode rays pass, it starts rotating. This proves that anode rays consist of fast-moving particles.
- **Anode rays are positively charged**: When an electric field is applied in the path of anode rays, they tend to bend towards the negatively charged plate. This proves that anode rays consist of positively charged particles and these particles are termed as **protons**.
- **Ratio of electric charge to mass (e/m) is not constant**: The charge (e) to mass (m) ratio of particles that constitute the anode rays is not constant and varies with the gases used in the discharge tube. This proves that the nature of anode rays produced depends on the gas used in the discharge tube.

Characteristics of a Proton

- The mass of a proton is equivalent to the mass of a hydrogen atom, which is about 1 atomic mass unit (a.m.u.) or 1.67×10^{-27} kg. It is about 1840 times heavier than an electron.
- Protons are particles with unit positive charge. The charge of a proton is $+1.6 \times 10^{-19}$ coulombs (C). It is equal in magnitude to the charge of an electron but opposite in sign.
- A proton is represented by the symbol $_1p^1$, where subscript '1' represents the mass and superscript '1' represents one unit positive charge.

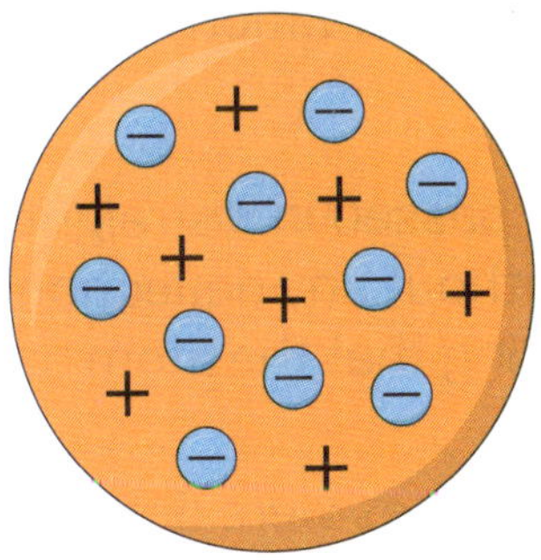

▲ Thomson's plum pudding model of the atom

Thomson's Plum Pudding Model

J. J. Thomson proposed the first model of an atom in 1904. It was called the **plum pudding model** of the atom and shows how the subatomic particles protons and electrons are arranged inside an atom. He theorized the atom to be a positively charged spherical substance in which negatively charged electrons are dispersed just like plums or raisins in a pudding. Although this model described that atoms are electrically neutral, his theory was later on proved to be wrong by his former student Rutherford.

Discovery of the Atomic Nucleus

In 1911, British physicist Lord Ernest Rutherford discovered that the nucleus is present at the centre of the atom while performing an experiment to find out the arrangement of protons and electrons inside an atom. This model is also known as the **nuclear atomic model**.

Rutherford's Alpha-Scattering Experiment

Rutherford conducted an experiment using the following materials:

- A source of alpha (α) particles – a radioactive substance in a lead container with an aperture to let the emitted radioactive particles escape in a desired direction

Do You Know?

An alpha particle is a helium nucleus. That is, it is a packet consisting of two protons and two neutrons with no electrons around it. Alpha particles are high-speed particles and can strongly interact with matter.

- A thin gold foil (1000 atoms thick)
- A detector of alpha particles – a screen coated with zinc sulphide which glows when α-particles strike it
- Rutherford placed the thin gold foil, surrounded by a zinc sulphide-coated screen, in the path of α-particles (positively charged helium ions). He bombarded the gold foil with α-particles.

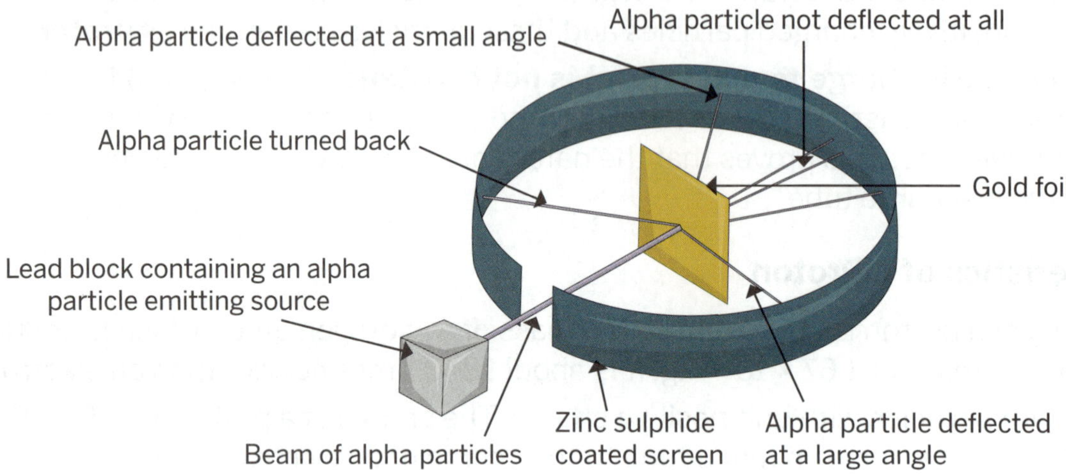

▲ Rutherford's alpha scattering experiment

Through this experiment, he expected that α-particles would be deflected by the subatomic particles in the gold foil, but he observed some unexpected results. His observations and the resulting conclusions are as follows:

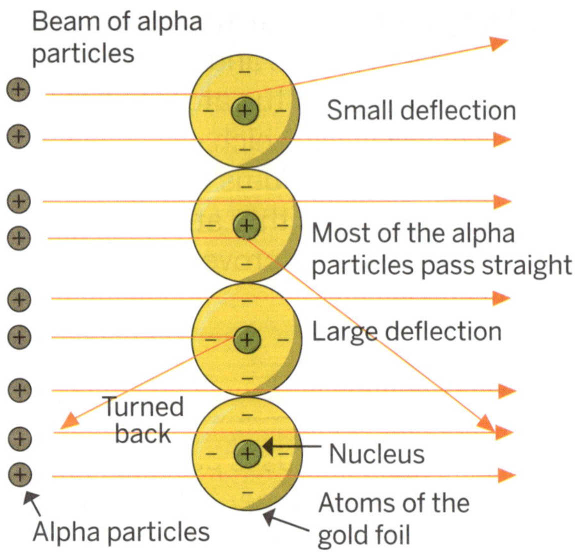

▲ Scattering of alpha particles through gold foil

- Most of the α-particles passed in a straight line through the gold foil without any deflection from their path, indicating that the atom has a lot of empty space in it.
- A small number of α-particles were deflected by small angles, indicating that they approached some positively charged region within the atom, which repelled the positively charged α-particles. This region was called the **nucleus** by Rutherford.
- A very small number of α-particles were deflected by large angles, indicating that they were repelled strongly by a central nucleus as all the mass and positive charge of an atom are concentrated in this very small region within the atom.

Rutherford's Model of Atom

Rutherford proposed the following model of an atom based on his alpha-scattering experiment.

- An atom has a positively charged region at its centre called the nucleus, which consists of protons (the positively charged particles).
- All the mass of an atom is concentrated in its nucleus.
- The size of the nucleus is very small as compared to the size of the atom.
- The electrons revolve around the nucleus in well-defined paths called **orbits** in the same way as the planets move around the Sun.

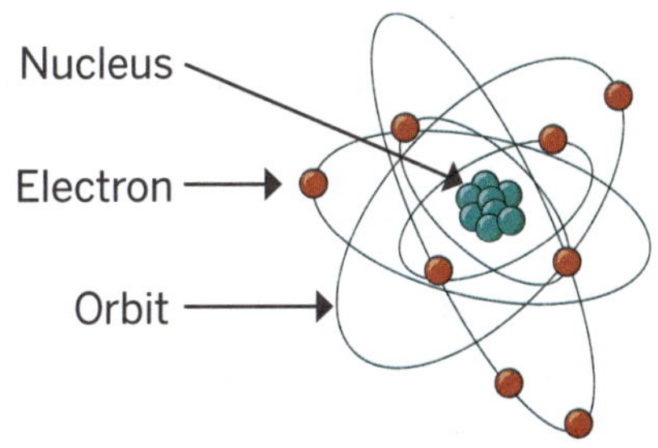

▲ Rutherford's model of atom

- The electrons and the nucleus are held together by a strong electrostatic force of attraction.
- An atom is electrically neutral. This implies that the number of electrons revolving around the nucleus should be equal to the number of protons, so as to neutralize the positive charge in the nucleus.

Drawbacks of Rutherford's Model of Atom

- His model failed to explain the exact arrangement of electrons in an atom and thus, the stability of the atom.
- As the electrons and the nucleus are held together by electrostatic forces of attraction, the electrons should fall into the nucleus eventually. But it does not happen and the atoms remain stable.

Discovery of Neutrons

Until 1920, an atom was considered to be the fundamental unit of matter, consisting of only positively charged protons and negatively charged electrons, thus making the atom electrically neutral.

Ernest Rutherford predicted the existence of another electrically neutral subatomic particle inside the nucleus of an atom with almost the same mass as the proton and called this particle the **neutral proton**. He thought that both protons and electrons might be very closely attached if they were the only particles present, as these were oppositely charged particles. But, as protons and electrons were not closely united, there should be another subatomic particle with no net charge.

Rutherford discussed this idea of neutral proton with his students, but no experimental evidence for neutral particles was obtained for many years. One of his students, James Chadwick made efforts to find this neutral proton and performed an experiment.

Chadwick's Experiment

Chadwick placed beryllium and polonium elements in a vacuum. Eventually, polonium emitted α-particles and these α-particles when made to hit beryllium, gave out mysterious particles.

> **Remember**
>
> **Electrons**: $_{-1}e^0$ — negligible mass and one unit negative charge
>
> **Protons**: $_1p^1$ — 1 a.m.u. mass and one unit positive charge
>
> **Neutrons**: $_0n^1$ — 1 a.m.u. mass and zero charge

He experimentally proved that these mysterious particles had the same mass as protons and were neutral in charge. Thus, Chadwick discovered this third subatomic particle in the year 1932 and named it **neutron**.

Characteristics of a Neutron

- The mass of a neutron is nearly equal to that of a proton, that is, 1 a.m.u.
- Neutrons are present in the nucleus of all atoms, with hydrogen being an exception, as it has no neutrons.
- A neutron does not have any charge.
- A neutron is represented by the symbol '$_0n^1$' where '0' represents the charge and '1' represents the mass.

Bohr's Model of Atom

To overcome the shortcomings of Rutherford's model, Danish physicist Neils Bohr postulated an atomic model. It is known as Bohr's model or the **extra-nuclear structure of atom**. He received the Nobel Prize in Physics in 1922 for his contribution towards this structure of atom. The significant features of the Bohr's atomic model are as follows:

- The electrons revolve around the nucleus in fixed paths called **orbits**, also known as **shells**.
- The shells or orbits are represented either by the numbers n = 1, 2, 3, 4, ... or by the letters K, L, M, N, ... (beginning from the innermost shell).

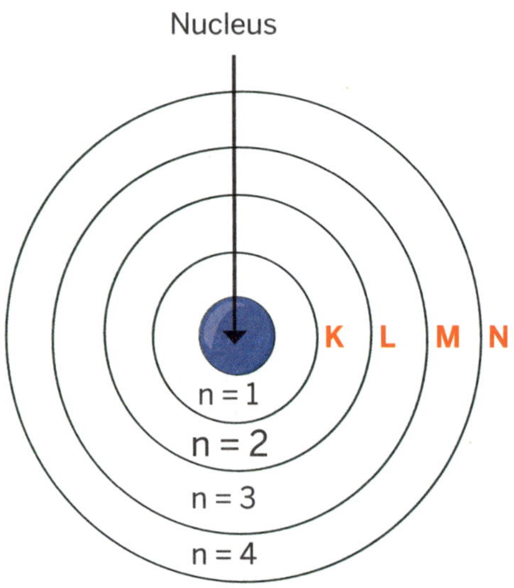

▲ Bohr's atomic model

- Each orbit or shell has a fixed amount of energy associated with it. Thus, the shells are also known as **energy levels** or **energy shells**. Energy of each shell increases as its distance from the nucleus increases.
- The first orbit from the nucleus (K-shell) has the lowest energy, the second orbit (L-shell) has a higher energy than the K-shell, the third orbit is the M-shell and has a higher energy than the L-shell and so on.
- Electrons will not lose energy as long as they are revolving in their particular energy level.
- Electrons lose energy when they move from a higher energy level to a lower energy level.

- Electrons gain energy when they move from a lower energy level to a higher energy level.
- The outermost shell of an atom is called its **valence shell**.

Revision Zone

Fill in the blanks.

1. Atoms ________ (can/cannot) be created or destroyed.
2. The charge to mass ratio of protons is ________ (constant/not constant).
3. Electrons ________ (gain/lose) energy when they move from a higher energy level to a lower energy level.
4. Neutrons were discovered by ________ (Rutherford/Chadwick).
5. The electrons and nucleus are held together by ________ (magnetic/electrostatic) forces of attraction.

Modern Concept of the Atom

As per the modern concept of the atom, an atom has the following features:

- An atom is made up of three subatomic particles: electrons, protons and neutrons.
- All the positive charge and mass of the atom is concentrated in a small volume in the centre which is called the nucleus.
- Protons and neutrons constitute the nucleus of the atom and are responsible for the entire mass of the atom.
- The nucleus is positively charged due to the presence of protons in it. Neutrons do not have any charge.
- Outside the nucleus, the electrons revolve in various fixed paths called orbits and do not contribute to the mass of the atom.
- Normally, an atom has equal number of electrons and protons, so it is electrically neutral in nature.

Atomic Number

Atomic number is defined as the number of protons present in the nucleus of an atom of an element. It is denoted by the letter Z.

$$\text{Atomic number } (Z) = \text{Number of protons } (p)$$

We know that the number of protons in the nucleus of an atom is equal to the number of electrons revolving around the nucleus of that atom.

That is,

Number of protons (p) = Number of electrons (e)

or, Atomic number (Z) = Number of protons (p) = Number of electrons (e)

Mass Number

Mass number is defined as the sum of the total number of protons and neutrons present in the nucleus of an atom of an element. It is denoted by the letter A. For example, the mass of the element aluminium is 27, which contains 13 protons and 14 neutrons.

Mass number (A) = Number of protons (p) + Number of neutrons (n)

If we know the mass number and atomic number of an element, the number of protons, electrons and neutrons in the atom of that element can be calculated.

Mass number (A) = Number of protons (p) + Number of neutrons (n)

Number of protons (p) = Atomic number (Z)

So, Mass number (A) = Atomic number (Z) + Number of neutrons (n)

or, Number of neutrons (n) = Mass number (A) – Atomic number (Z)

Table 4.1 Atomic number and mass number of some elements

Element	Atomic number	Mass number	Number of neutrons
Caesium (Cs)	55	132	77
Copper (Cu)	29	63	34
Palladium (Pd)	46	106	60
Iodine (I)	53	126	73
Sulphur (S)	16	32	16
Antimony (Sb)	51	121	70
Cadmium (Cd)	48	112	64
Iron (Fe)	26	55	29

The representation of the mass number and atomic number of an element along with the symbol of that element is called its **atomic notation**.

An element is represented by ${}^{A}_{Z}X$ or ${}_{Z}X^{A}$ where X is the chemical symbol of the element, A is the mass number and Z is the atomic number. For example, helium, carbon and sulphur can be written as ${}^{4}_{2}He$ or ${}_{2}He^{4}$, ${}^{12}_{6}C$ or ${}_{6}C^{12}$ and ${}^{32}_{16}S$ or ${}_{16}S^{32}$, respectively.

Electronic Configuration

The systematic distribution or arrangement of electrons in various orbits or shells around the nucleus of an atom is called **electronic configuration**. It was explained by the scientists **Bohr** and **Bury**. The main rules suggested by them are known as **Bohr–Bury rules** and are given by:

- The maximum number of electrons that can be accommodated in a given shell or orbit is $2n^2$ where n is the number of the energy shell.
- The maximum number of electrons that can be accommodated in the outermost or valence shell is 8, except for the K-shell (if it is the outermost shell) as it can hold only a maximum of 2 electrons. The shell just before the valence shell can hold only a maximum of 18 electrons.

Table 4.2 gives the maximum number of electrons in various shells.

- The electrons will first try to occupy the shell that contains the lowest energy. Electrons will not try to occupy the next shell until the lowest energy shells are filled.
- If the outermost shell is K-shell and is filled with the maximum of two electrons, it is referred to as **duplet configuration**. In all the other cases, if the outermost shell is filled with the maximum of eight electrons, it is referred to as **octet configuration**. The atom of an element that has a duplet or an octet configuration is considered to be stable as compared to other elements that do not have these configurations. Table 4.3 gives the electronic configuration of the first 20 elements.

Table 4.2 Maximum number of electrons in various shells

Shell or orbit name	Shell number, n	Maximum no. of electrons, $2n^2$
K-shell	1	$2 \times 1^2 = 2$
L-shell	2	$2 \times 2^2 = 8$
M-shell	3	$2 \times 3^2 = 18$
N-shell	4	$2 \times 4^2 = 32$

Table 4.3 Electronic configuration of the first 20 elements

Element	Symbol	Atomic no. (*Z*)	Mass no. (*A*)	No. of protons	No. of electrons	No. of neutrons (*A* – *Z*)	Electronic configuration			
							K	L	M	N
Hydrogen	H	1	1	1	1	1 – 1 = 0	1			
Helium	He	2	4	2	2	4 – 2 = 2	2			
Lithium	Li	3	7	3	3	7 – 3 = 4	2	1		
Beryllium	Be	4	9	4	4	9 – 4 = 5	2	2		
Boron	B	5	11	5	5	11 – 5 = 6	2	3		
Carbon	C	6	12	6	6	12 – 6 = 6	2	4		
Nitrogen	N	7	14	7	7	14 – 7 = 7	2	5		
Oxygen	O	8	16	8	8	16 – 8 = 8	2	6		
Fluorine	F	9	19	9	9	19 – 9 = 10	2	7		
Neon	Ne	10	20	10	10	20 – 10 = 10	2	8		
Sodium	Na	11	23	11	11	23 – 11 = 12	2	8	1	
Magnesium	Mg	12	24	12	12	24 – 12= 12	2	8	2	
Aluminium	Al	13	27	13	13	27 – 13 = 14	2	8	3	
Silicon	Si	14	28	14	14	28 – 14 = 14	2	8	4	
Phosphorus	P	15	31	15	15	31 – 15 = 16	2	8	5	
Sulphur	S	16	32	16	16	32 – 16 = 16	2	8	6	
Chlorine	Cl	17	35	17	17	35 – 17 = 18	2	8	7	
Argon	Ar	18	40	18	18	40 – 18 = 22	2	8	8	
Potassium	K	19	39	19	19	39 – 19 = 20	2	8	8	1
Calcium	Ca	20	40	20	20	40 – 20 = 20	2	8	8	2

The arrangement of electrons for the first 20 elements are illustrated as follows.

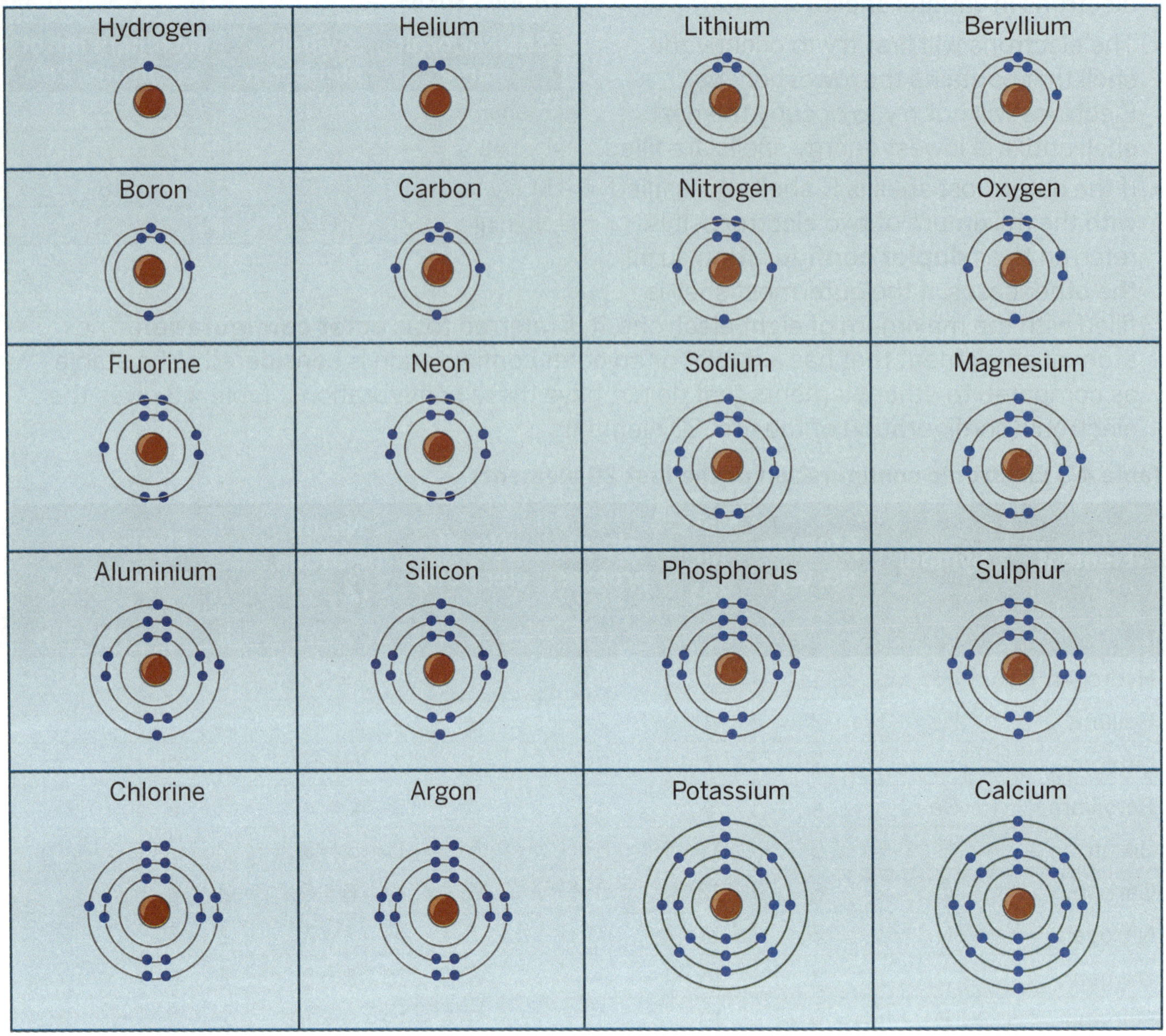

Valency

The combining capacity of the atom of an element with other atoms or elements is known as its **valency**. It can also be defined as the number of electrons an atom can donate or accept in order to combine chemically with other atoms or elements and form molecules or compounds.

Every atom tries to achieve an octet (or duplet) configuration by either accepting/gaining or donating/losing valence electrons (electrons in the valence shell) to become stable. Valence electrons are the ones which take part in chemical reactions and result in the formation of different molecules or compounds.

Science in Context

Elements that have eight electrons in their outermost shell or orbit are inactive and do not mostly take part in chemical reactions. These elements are called **inert gases** or **noble gases**, for example, neon and argon.

Valency of an element is always a whole number. We can determine the valency of an element by knowing its electronic configuration. Let us find out.

- Elements of metals have 1, 2 or 3 valence electrons in their valence shell. Thus, they tend to donate or lose electrons in order to achieve the octet configuration of 8 valence electrons. So, the valency of a metal is calculated as the number of valence electrons in the valence shell of its atom. For example, the electronic configuration of sodium is 2, 8, 1. It has one valence electron and hence its valency is 1.
- Elements of non-metals have 5, 6 or 7 valence electrons. Thus, they tend to accept or gain electrons in order to achieve the octet configuration of 8 valence electrons. So, the valency of a non-metal is 8 – the number of valence electrons. For example, the electronic configuration of chlorine is 2, 8, 7. It has 7 valence electrons and requires only one electron to complete its valence shell. Hence, its valency is 1 (8 – 7 = 1).
- Elements of noble or inert gases have a valency of 0 as their valence shells are already complete with 8 electrons. For example, helium has 2 valence electrons (duplet configuration) and neon has 8 valence electrons (octet configuration).

Table 4.4 Valencies of some elements

Element	Valency
Sodium	1 (monovalent)
Potassium	1 (monovalent)
Silver	1 (monovalent)
Zinc	2 (divalent)

Element	Valency
Magnesium	2 (divalent)
Calcium	2 (divalent)
Aluminium	3 (trivalent)
Hydrogen	1 (monovalent)

Element	Valency
Chlorine	1 (monovalent)
Carbon	4 (tetravalent)
Oxygen	2 (divalent)
Iodine	1 (monovalent)

The valency of an element can also be defined as the number of hydrogen atoms that can combine or replace either indirectly or directly with one atom of the element. The valency of hydrogen is 1 (monovalent).

Variable Valency

Some elements exhibit more than one valency as their atoms have different combining capacities while forming molecules or compounds. That is, atoms of such elements can donate or accept different number of electrons depending upon the conditions. Hence, they are said to have variable valency. For example, iron can have valencies 2 and 3. In ferrous chloride ($FeCl_2$), the valency of iron is 2, whereas in ferric chloride ($FeCl_3$), its valency is 3.

Table 4.5 Variable valencies of some elements

Element	Variable valencies	Representation
Copper	1, 2	Cu (I), Cu (II)
Iron	2, 3	Fe (II), Fe (III)
Silver	1, 2	Ag (I), Ag (II)
Mercury	1, 2	Hg (I), Hg (II)
Nickel	2, 3, 4	Ni (II), Ni (III), Ni (IV)

Elements with variable valency are represented by writing the symbol of the element followed by its valency in Roman numerals within brackets. For example, Fe (II), Fe (III), Ca (I), Ca (II), etc.

Ions and Radicals

We studied that atoms are neutral (that is, they do not carry any charge) as the number of protons present inside the nucleus is equal to the number of electrons that revolve around the nucleus. However, when an atom donates or accepts one or more of electrons, this equality or balance is lost and the atom acquires a positive or negative charge. For example, when a sodium atom loses an electron, it acquires a positive charge (Na^+) as the number of protons in it becomes more than the number of electrons. Similarly, when a chlorine atom accepts an electron, it acquires a negative charge (Cl^-) as the number of electrons in it becomes more than the number of protons.

An atom that attains a positive or a negative charge as a result of loss or gain of electrons is called an **ion**. The atom that donates or loses electrons attains a positive charge and is called a **cation** or positive ion. Examples of cations are potassium (K^+), calcium (Ca^{2+}) and zinc (Zn^{2+}). The atom that accepts or gains electrons attains a negative charge and is called an **anion** or negative ion. Examples of anions are bromide (Br^-), oxide (O^{2-}) and sulphide (S^{2-}).

An atom or a group of atoms of different elements that behaves as a single unit and carries a positive or negative charge is called a **radical**. A radical may contain one or more kinds of atoms. For example, zinc (Zn^{2+}) and sodium (Na^+) radicals contain only one kind of atoms; hence, these are called **simple radicals**. Carbonate $(CO_3)^{2-}$ and sulphate $(SO_4)^{2-}$ radicals contain two kinds of atoms each; hence, these are called **compound radicals.**

Table 4.6 Some radicals and their symbols

Name of the radical	Symbol	Name of the radical	Symbol
Hydrogen	H^+	Hydride	H^-
Iron (II)	Fe^{2+}	Oxide	O^{2-}
Aluminium	Al^{3+}	Nitrate	NO_3^-
Magnesium	Mg^{2+}	Hydroxide	OH^-
Copper	Cu^{2+}	Hydrogen carbonate	HCO_3^-
Ammonium	NH_4^+	Phosphate	PO_4^{3-}

Radicals cannot exist independently and thus always combine with other radicals or elements. For example, carbonate is a compound radical with the formula CO_3^{2-}. It cannot exist independently and thus combines with other radicals like Ca^{2+} to form a compound, calcium carbonate ($CaCO_3$). The compound calcium carbonate ($CaCO_3$) contains two radicals: one is the positive radical Ca^{2+} and the other is the negative radical CO_3^{2-}, where both radicals have the valency 2.

Revision Zone

Match the elements with their valencies.

1. Aluminium	a. Monovalent
2. Magnesium	b. Tetravalent
3. Chlorine	c. Divalent
4. Carbon	d. Trivalent

Keywords

Paramanu: a particle that cannot be further divided

Protons: the subatomic particles present in the nucleus of an atom with a unit positive charge and mass equal to that of a hydrogen atom

Electrons: the subatomic particles that revolve around the nucleus of an atom with a unit negative charge and mass equal to 1/1837 times that of a hydrogen atom

Neutrons: the subatomic particles present in the nucleus of an atom that do not have any charge and have mass nearly equal to that of a proton

Atomic number: the number protons present in the nucleus of an atom of an element

Mass number: the sum of the number of protons and neutrons in the nucleus of an atom of an element

Electronic configuration: the systematic distribution or arrangement of electrons in various orbits or shells around the nucleus of an atom

Valency: the combining capacity of the atom of an element with other atoms or elements

In a Nutshell

- Maharshi Kanada (600 BC) proposed that matter consists of indivisible particles and he referred to them as paramanu.
- Democritus (400 BC) stated that matter is made up of atoms and these atoms are invisible and indivisible.
- John Dalton stated that matter is composed of tiny particles called atoms, which are indivisible and cannot be created or destroyed.
- Electrons are subatomic particles with unit negative charge and mass 1/1837 times that of a hydrogen atom. They were discovered by J. J. Thomson.
- Protons are subatomic particles with mass equal to that of a hydrogen atom and unit positive charge. They were discovered by Eugen Goldstein.
- In 1911, Lord Ernest Rutherford discovered that a nucleus is present in the atom through his alpha-scattering experiment.
- Neutrons are subatomic particles without any charge and have mass nearly equal to that of protons. They were discovered by the scientist J. Chadwick.
- Nucleus is the central part of the atom in which all the positive charge and mass is concentrated in a small volume.
- The Neils Bohr model of the atom states that electrons revolve around the nucleus in fixed orbits. The shells or orbits are represented by the numbers n = 1, 2, 3, 4, ... or by the letters K, L, M, N, ...

Exercise

1 Choose the correct answer for each of the following.

a. Rutherford's alpha-scattering experiment led to the discovery of
   i. protons ii. electrons
   iii. neutrons iv. nucleus

b. Element X consists of 18 protons and 19 neutrons. Which of these is the correct depiction of the atom?
   i. ${}_{18}X^{37}$ ii. ${}_{37}X^{18}$
   iii. ${}_{18}X^{19}$ iv. ${}_{19}X^{18}$

c. The mass of an atom is determined by the sum of the masses of
   i. electrons
   ii. neutrons
   iii. neutrons and protons
   iv. electrons and neutrons

d. Valency of oxygen is
   i. 1 ii. 2
   iii. 3 iv. 4

e. Which of the following elements shows variable valency?
   i. Nickel ii. Sodium
   iii. Helium iv. Carbon

2 Fill in the blanks.

a. The maximum number of electrons that can be accommodated in the outermost orbit is ____________ (8/18).

b. The total number of protons present in the nucleus of an atom is referred to as the __________ (atomic number/ mass number).

c. Electrons were discovered by ________________ (Bohr/Thomson).

d. The positively charged centre of an atom is called the ___________ (nucleus/proton).

e. The electrons present in the outer most shell of an atom are known as ______________ (charged electrons/ valence electrons).

f. Hydrogen atom does not have _____________ (protons/neutrons).

3 Write T for True and F for False.

a. In the gold foil experiment, cathode rays produced a green glow at the other end of the tube.

b. The mass of an electron is about 1/2000 times that of a hydrogen atom.

c. The number of protons and electrons is always same in a neutral atom.

d. The fixed circular paths around the nucleus are called orbits.

e. An element has five electrons in the M-shell. The atomic number of the element is 15.

f. Neils Bohr proposed that electrons are distributed in different shells around the nucleus.

g. The number of valence electrons in nitrogen is three.

4 Answer the following questions in one line each.

a. Who suggested the distribution of electrons in different orbits of an atom?

b. What is the electronic configuration of an atom that has a proton number of 5 and a mass number of 11?

c. Name the scientist who discovered anode rays.

d. Give two examples of a compound radical.

e. Write the atomic notation of the element X that consists of 19 protons and 20 neutrons.

5. **Define the following terms.**
   a. Mass number
   b. Variable valency
   c. Atomic number
   d. Anode rays
   e. Electronic configuration

6. **Differentiate between the following.**
   a. Electrons and protons
   b. Anode rays and cathode rays
   c. Atomic number and mass number
   d. Ion and radical
   e. Simple radical and compound radical

7. **Answer the following questions in brief.**
   a. Represent diagrammatically the electronic configuration of the element magnesium.
   b. An element consists of 15 protons and 16 neutrons. Mention the number of electrons, atomic number and mass number of this element.
   c. Mention any four postulates of Dalton's atomic theory.
   d. What is Thomson's plum pudding model?
   e. What is valency? Explain it with an example.

8. **Answer the following questions in detail.**
   a. Explain the discovery of electrons.
   b. Explain Rutherford's alpha-scattering experiment and the conclusions drawn from it.
   c. Explain the discovery of protons by Eugen Goldstein.
   d. Explain the arrangement of electrons in an atom by Bohr–Bury.
   e. Explain the discovery of neutrons.

9. **Think and answer.**

   What happens to the flow (number and speed) of electrons if we introduce two anodes at one end of the cathode?

   (Hint: Recall the concept of J. J. Thomson cathode ray experiment.)

10. **Project**

    Draw a timeline to show how the atomic theory has developed over the past several hundred years.

11. **In the Library**

    Collect information about elements prepared in the lab synthetically and their inventors.

Worksheet

Subject Integration

Look at the J.J. Thomson's cathode ray experimental set-up shown below and answer the questions that follow.

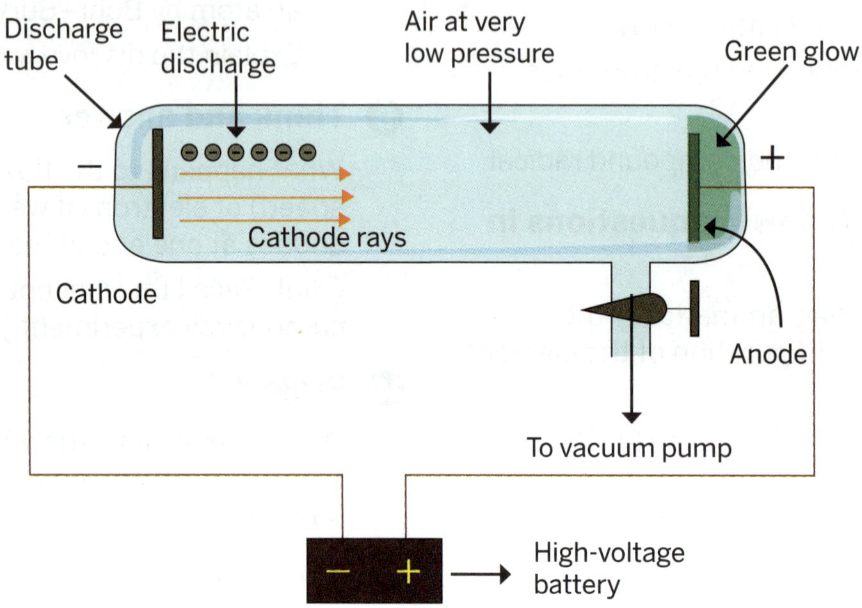

a. What is the use of vacuum pump in the above experiment?

____

____

b. What was the reason for passing high voltage and maintaining low pressure conditions in the above experiment?

____

____

c. What would happen if the experiment was carried out under normal conditions (normal voltage and normal pressure)?

____

____

d. How did Thomson conclude that cathode rays consist of negatively charged particles and term them as 'electrons'?

____

____

____

Language of Chemistry

5

Introduction

What I shall learn

- Representation of elements
- Representation of compounds
- Write chemical equation of a reaction
- Balance chemical equations

We use a variety of substances in our daily life. Each substance around us is made of matter. From the food we eat to the water we drink to the air we breathe and all the non-living objects are made of matter. We know that each substance has a unique composition. We also know that chemical changes are caused by the chemical reactions that take place during a chemical change. In this chapter, we will revise and learn more about chemical reactions.

Elements

A substance that consists of only one kind of atoms is called an **element**. The smallest unit of an element is an atom. For example, the element gold contains only one kind of atoms, that is, gold atoms. Other examples of elements are carbon, sodium and oxygen. We know that all the atoms that make up an element are of the same kind, but two different elements cannot have the same kind of atoms. For instance, atoms of oxygen and atoms of hydrogen are different from each other. So, every element has its own unique properties.

So far, nearly 118 elements have been discovered. Of these, 98 elements are found naturally on Earth and the remaining 20 elements have been prepared artificially by scientists in laboratories.

Characteristics of Elements

- Elements are pure substances that consist of only one kind of atoms.
- Each element has its own unique properties.
- The atoms of an element exhibit the same properties as the element.
- Elements cannot be separated or broken down into simpler components by physical or chemical methods.

Representation of Elements

Elements or atoms of an element are represented using symbols. The representation of an element using the short form or abbreviation of its name is known as its **chemical symbol**.

In earlier times, the elements were represented pictorially. Later, the elements were named after the name of the place where they were first found. For example, the name copper and its symbol Cu come from the Latin word *cuprum*, which means 'from the island of Cyprus'. In the modern method of representing elements, letters representing the names of the elements are used as symbols.

Features of the modern method of representation are as follows.

- The first letter of the name of the element is used as the symbol. The first letter is written as a capital letter. For example, H for hydrogen, O for oxygen and C for carbon. The English names of these elements are similar to their Latin names.
- If two or more elements have their English names starting with the same letter, then a two-letter symbol is used. The first letter of the name is the first letter of the symbol and the next non-repeating letter of the name is the second letter of the symbol. The first letter is written as a capital letter and the second letter is written as a small letter. For example, Ca for calcium, Cd for cadmium, Cl for chlorine and Co for cobalt.
- In some cases, the English names and the Latin names of the elements are different. So, for these elements, the symbols are derived from their Latin names. For example, the Latin name of potassium is *kalium* and its symbol is K. Similarly, the Latin name of gold is *aurum* and its symbol is Au.

Table 5.1 Some elements and their symbols

Element	Symbol	Element	Symbol
Helium	He	Phosphorus	P
Nitrogen	N	Magnesium	Mg
Iodine	I	Manganese	Mn
Aluminium	Al	Argon	Ar
Zinc	Zn	Platinum	Pt

Table 5.2 Some elements with their Latin names and symbols

Element	Latin name	Symbol
Sodium	*Natrium*	Na
Iron	*Ferrum*	Fe
Copper	*Cuprum*	Cu
Silver	*Argentum*	Ag
Mercury	*Hydrargyrum*	Hg

Know the Scientist

J J Berzelius (1779–1848) was a Swedish chemist who made several contributions to the field of chemistry. He was the first person to suggest that the first one or two letters of the names of elements can be used as symbols. He identified the elements thorium, silicon, cerium and selenium. He is popularly known as the father of Swedish chemistry.

Compounds

The chemical substance formed when two or more atoms of different elements combine chemically in a fixed proportion is called a **compound**. A compound is made up of molecules of the same kind. For example, water contains only one kind of molecules, that is, water molecules. Other examples of compounds are carbon dioxide, salt and sugar.

Characteristics of Compounds

- Compounds are pure substances formed when two or more atoms of different elements combine together chemically in a fixed proportion.
- The properties of compounds are different from the properties of their constituent elements.
- Compounds exhibit their own physical and chemical properties.
- Compounds can be separated into their individual components by chemical methods.

Representation of Compounds

Just as we represent elements by their chemical symbols, compounds can be represented by chemical formulae. A chemical formula is the representation of a compound using the symbols of its constituent elements. In other words, the symbolic representation of the composition of a chemical compound is known as its **chemical formula**.

A chemical formula exhibits the different elements present in a molecule of a compound and the number of atoms of each combining or constituent element it contains. For example, the chemical formula of carbon dioxide is CO_2. This indicates that a molecule of CO_2 consists of one atom of carbon and two atoms of oxygen.

We can easily write the chemical formula of a compound if we know the symbols and valencies of atoms of the different elements forming the compound.

Follow the steps given below to write the chemical formula of a compound.

1. Write the symbols of the elements or radicals/ions that form the compound.
2. The metallic part (positive ion) of the compound should always be written first followed by the non-metallic part (negative ion).
3. Write their valencies on top of their symbols as superscripts.
4. If the valencies are identical, cancel the valencies. If the valencies are different, then interchange the valencies with respect to the symbols by making arrows and write them as subscripts.
5. Simplify the formula by dividing the valencies by a common factor, if divisible.
6. If the compound contains compound radicals, then the radicals are enclosed in brackets and the number is written outside the brackets as subscript. For instance, the valency of magnesium (Mg^{2+}) is two and that of nitrate (NO_3^-) is one. Thus, the chemical formula of magnesium nitrate is written as $Mg(NO_3)_2$.
7. The valency 1 need not be written in the final formula.

Find Out

Why is it important to know the valencies to write a chemical formula?

Keeping in mind the above steps, let us write the chemical formulae of some compounds.

Writing the Formulae of Chlorides

Calcium chloride

Step 1: Ca Cl (Write the symbols of the constituent elements, here calcium and chlorine)

Step 2: Ca^2 Cl^1 (Write the valency of each element as superscript)

Step 3: Ca^2 Cl^1 (Interchange the valencies and write them as subscripts)

Ca_1 Cl_2

Step 4: Ca_1 Cl_2 (Divide the valencies by a common factor, if divisible)

Chemical formula of calcium chloride: $CaCl_2$ (Valency 1 need not be written)

Table 5.3 Some metallic chlorides and their chemical formulae

Compound	Formula
Sodium chloride	$NaCl$
Potassium chloride	KCl
Magnesium chloride	$MgCl_2$
Copper chloride	$CuCl_2$
Zinc chloride	$ZnCl_2$

Writing the Formulae of Oxides

Magnesium oxide

Step 1: Mg O

Step 2: Mg^2 O^2

Step 3: Mg^2 O^2

Mg_2 O_2

Step 4: Mg_2 O_2 (Divide the valencies by a common factor, here 2)

Mg_1 O_1

Chemical formula of magnesium oxide: MgO

Table 5.4 Some metallic oxides and their chemical formulae

Compound	Formula
Sodium oxide	Na_2O
Calcium oxide	CaO
Zinc oxide	ZnO
Copper oxide	CuO
Potassium oxide	K_2O

Writing the Formulae of Sulphides

Sodium sulphide

Step 1: Na S

Step 2: Na^1 S^2

Step 3: Na^1 S^2

Na_2 S_1

Step 4: Na_2 S_1

Chemical formula of sodium sulphide: Na_2S

Table 5.5 Some metallic sulphides and their chemical formulae

Compound	Formula
Zinc sulphide	ZnS
Ferric sulphide	Fe_2S_3
Hydrogen sulphide	H_2S
Calcium sulphide	CaS
Copper sulphide	Cu_2S

Remember

In a chemical formula, the subscript denotes the number of atoms of the element present in one molecule of the compound. For example, in Fe_2S_3, there are 2 atoms of iron and 3 atoms of sulphur.

Table 5.6 Some compounds with their constituent elements and chemical formulae

Compound	Constituent elements	Formula	Compound	Constituent elements	Formula
Methane	Carbon (C) Hydrogen(H)	CH_4	Sulphur dioxide	Sulphur (S) Oxygen (O)	SO_2
Sodium hydroxide	Sodium (Na) Oxygen (O) Hydrogen (H)	NaOH	Sulphuric acid	Hydrogen (H) Sulphur (S) Oxygen (O)	H_2SO_4
Calcium hydroxide	Calcium (Ca) Oxygen (O) Hydrogen (H)	$Ca(OH)_2$	Copper sulphate	Copper (Cu) Sulphur (S) Oxygen (O)	$CuSO_4$
Potassium nitrate	Potassium (K) Nitrogen (N) Oxygen (O)	KNO_3	Calcium carbonate	Calcium (Ca) Carbon (C) Oxygen (O)	$CaCO_3$

Revision Zone

Match the compounds with their chemical formulae.

1. Copper chloride	a. CaS
2. Zinc oxide	b. $CuCl_2$
3. Sodium oxide	c. ZnO
4. Calcium sulphide	d. Na_2O

Chemical Reactions

A chemical change in which one or more substances react or combine together resulting in the formation of one or more new substances is called a **chemical reaction**. In a chemical reaction, atoms or group of atoms of the original substance(s) basically rearrange themselves to form new substances.

In this rearrangement process, either two or more substances combine with each other to form new substances or a substance may separate into two or more new substances. In other words, a chemical reaction is a process in which chemical bonds between the combining substances are broken down and new bonds are formed by rearranging atoms in order to produce new substances.

Representation of Chemical Reactions

The representation of a chemical reaction using symbols and formulae of the elements or compounds involved in the reaction is known as a **chemical equation**. The chemical substances that participate in a chemical reaction are known as **reactants**. The new substances formed during a chemical reaction are known as **products**.

For example, consider the reaction of magnesium with oxygen. Magnesium reacts with oxygen to form magnesium oxide. The word equation of the chemical reaction is:

$$\text{Magnesium} + \text{Oxygen} \longrightarrow \text{Magnesium oxide}$$

The word equation indicates the change of reactants to products through an arrow placed between them. The reactants are written on the left-hand side, and the combination is shown with a plus sign (+) between them. The products are written on the right-hand side. If there is more than one product, then a plus sign is written between the products. The head of the arrow points towards the products, which conveys the direction of the reaction. To write a chemical equation, the names of the reactants and the products are replaced with their symbols and formulae.

$$Mg + O_2 \longrightarrow MgO$$

The number of atoms of each element on both sides of the equation should be equal (as per the law of conservation of mass, which states that mass is neither created nor destroyed), that is, the equation should be balanced.

$$\underbrace{\underset{\text{Magnesium}}{2Mg} + \underset{\text{Oxygen}}{O_2}}_{\text{(Reactants)}} \longrightarrow \underset{\text{(Product)}}{\underset{\text{Magnesium oxide}}{2MgO}}$$

Law of Conservation of Mass

The law of conservation of mass states that mass in an isolated system can neither be created nor be destroyed by chemical reactions or physical transformations. Hence, during a chemical reaction, the atoms are only rearranged to provide new products. The rearrangement of atoms happens in such a way that the total mass of the reactants is equal to the total mass of the products, provided masses are measured under similar conditions. In other words, the number of atoms of each element in the reactants and the products remains the same.

For example, if A and B react to form C and D, then according to the law of conservation of mass:

$$\text{Mass of A} + \text{Mass of B} = \text{Mass of C} + \text{Mass of D}$$

i.e., the total mass of the reactants should be equal to the total mass of the products formed in the reaction.

Molecular Mass

Molecular mass is expressed in the unit a.m.u. It is the total average atomic mass of all the atoms of a molecule.

Table 5.7 Atomic masses of some elements

Element	Atomic mass	Element	Atomic mass	Element	Atomic mass
Lithium	6.9	Neon	20.2	Chlorine	35.4
Beryllium	9.0	Sodium	23.0	Potassium	39.1

Element	Atomic mass
Boron	10.8
Carbon	12.0
Nitrogen	14.0
Oxygen	16.0
Fluorine	19.0

Element	Atomic mass
Magnesium	24.3
Aluminium	27.0
Silicon	28.1
Phosphorus	31.0
Sulphur	32.1

Element	Atomic mass
Argon	39.9
Calcium	40.0
Bromine	79.9
Strontium	87.6
Iodine	126.9

Calculation of molecular mass of MgO (magnesium oxide)

Atomic mass of magnesium = 24.3

Atomic mass of oxygen = 16

So, the molecular mass of magnesium oxide (MgO) = $1 \times 24.3 + 1 \times 16 = 40.3$ a.m.u.

Calculation of molecular mass of $CaCO_3$ (calcium carbonate)

Atomic mass of calcium = 40

Atomic mass of carbon = 12

Atomic mass of oxygen = 16

So, the molecular mass of calcium carbonate ($CaCO_3$) = $1 \times 40 + 1 \times 12 + 3 \times 16 = 100$ a.m.u.

Solved Problems

1. Calculate the amount of oxygen gas required and magnesium oxide formed when 60 g of magnesium is burned completely in oxygen.

Solution:

- The balanced chemical equation for the reaction of magnesium and oxygen is

$$2Mg + O_2 \longrightarrow 2MgO$$

- The total mass of the products and reactants should be calculated.
  Atomic mass of magnesium = 24.3; Atomic mass of oxygen = 16
  So, the mass equation can be written as

$$2 \times 24.3 + 2 \times 16 \longrightarrow 2(24.3 + 16)$$

$$48.6\text{ g} + 32\text{ g} \longrightarrow 80.6\text{ g}$$

- Oxygen needed to burn 48.6 g of magnesium is 32 g.
  Oxygen needed to burn 60 g of magnesium is = $(32/48.6) \times 60 = 39.5$ g
- Magnesium oxide formed by burning 48.6 g of magnesium = 80.6 g
  Magnesium oxide formed by burning 60 g of magnesium = $(80.6/48.6) \times 60 = 99.5$ g

Thus, when 60 g of magnesium is burned completely in oxygen, 39.5 g of oxygen is required and 99.5 g of magnesium oxide is formed.

2. Calculate the amount of carbon dioxide gas and calcium oxide (quick lime) formed during the decomposition of 25 g of calcium carbonate (limestone).

Solution:

- The balanced chemical equation for the decomposition of calcium carbonate is

$$CaCO_3 \longrightarrow CaO + CO_2$$

- The total mass of the products and reactants should be calculated.
  Atomic mass of calcium = 40; Atomic mass of oxygen = 16; Atomic mass of carbon = 12
  So, the mass equation can be written as

$$40 + 12 + (16 \times 3) \longrightarrow 40 + 16 + 12 + (2 \times 16)$$

$$100\text{ g} \longrightarrow 56\text{ g} + 44\text{ g}$$

- 100 g of $CaCO_3$ on decomposition forms = 56 g of CaO
  25 g of $CaCO_3$ on decomposition forms = (56/100) × 25 g = 14 g CaO
- 100 g of $CaCO_3$ on decomposition forms = 44 g of CO_2
  25 g of $CaCO_3$ on decomposition forms = (44/100) × 25 g = 11 g CO_2

Thus, on decomposition of 25 g of calcium carbonate, 11 g of carbon dioxide gas and 14 g of calcium oxide are formed.

Balancing a Chemical Equation

Consider the reaction of magnesium with oxygen.

$$Mg + O_2 \longrightarrow MgO$$

1. Count the number of atoms of each element in the reactants and products.

Element	Number of atoms in reactants (LHS)	Number of atoms in products (RHS)
Mg (Magnesium)	1	1
O (Oxygen)	2	1

From the above table, we can see that one atom of magnesium and two atoms of oxygen take part in the reaction to form one molecule of magnesium oxide. But one oxygen atom is enough to react with magnesium atom to form one molecule of magnesium oxide. Oxygen cannot be destroyed. So, if there are two oxygen atoms participating in a reaction, each will need a magnesium atom. So, we balance the equation to show the correct number of atoms participating in the reaction. How do we do that?

2. To balance the oxygen atoms on both sides of the equation, multiply the product (RHS) by 2.

Element	Number of atoms in reactants (LHS)	Number of atoms in products (RHS)
Mg (Magnesium)	1	$1 \times 2 = 2$
O (Oxygen)	2	$1 \times 2 = 2$

$$Mg + O_2 \longrightarrow 2MgO$$

Now, in the equation, the number of oxygen atoms is balanced but the number of magnesium atoms on both the sides is not balanced.

3. To balance the magnesium atoms on both sides of the equation, multiply the magnesium in the reactants (LHS) by 2.

Element	Number of atoms in reactants (LHS)	Number of atoms in products (RHS)
Mg (Magnesium)	$1 \times 2 = 2$	$1 \times 2 = 2$
O (Oxygen)	2	$1 \times 2 = 2$

$$2Mg + O_2 \longrightarrow 2MgO$$

The chemical equation, thus obtained, is said to be balanced.

The physical states of the reactants and products are mentioned along with their chemical formulae to make a chemical equation more informative.

The following notations are used to indicate the physical states of matter.

- (g) for gaseous substances
- (s) for solids
- (l) for liquids
- (aq) if the reactant or product is present as a solution in water
- (↑) If the reactant or product is a gas
- (↓) If the reactant or product is a precipitate

The state of matter is written next to the formula of the substance as given in the following equation.

$$\underset{\text{Zinc}}{Zn\,(s)} + \underset{\text{Hydrochloric Acid}}{2HCl\,(aq)} \longrightarrow \underset{\text{Zinc Chloride}}{ZnCl_2(aq)} + \underset{\text{Hydrogen}}{H_2(g)\,(\uparrow)}$$

Sometimes the reaction conditions such as temperature, heat, pressure, catalyst, etc., for the reaction are indicated above and/or below the arrow in the chemical equations.

$$\underset{\text{Silver Chloride}}{2AgCl(s)} \xrightarrow{\text{sunlight}} \underset{\text{Silver}}{2Ag(s)} + \underset{\text{Chlorine}}{Cl_2(g)}$$

$$\underset{\text{Carbon Monoxide}}{CO(g)} + \underset{\text{Hydrogen}}{2H_2(g)} \xrightarrow{\text{340 atm}} \underset{\text{Methanol}}{CH_3OH(l)}$$

$$\underset{\text{Carbon Dioxide}}{6CO_2(g)} + \underset{\text{Water}}{6H_2O\,(l)} \xrightarrow{\text{sunlight}} \underset{\text{Glucose}}{C_6H_{12}O_6(s)} + \underset{\text{Oxygen}}{6O_2(g)}$$

What do Balanced Chemical Equations Convey?

We can get the following information by looking at a balanced chemical equation:

- The reactants that take part in the reaction and the products that are formed along with their symbols and formulae
- The physical state of the reactants and products along with the conditions required for the chemical reaction

- The number of molecules of the reactants and the products that take part in the reaction
- The number of atoms of each element of the reactants and the products that take part in the reaction
- Help in determining the mass of the reactants and the products

Limitations of Chemical Equations

- A chemical equation does not reveal if the reaction is complete or incomplete.
- It does not mention the speed of the reaction.
- It does not give the concentration of the substances.
- It does not give the conditions of temperature, pressure, catalyst, etc. This is overcome by mentioning these above or below the arrow.
- It does not give any idea about colour changes, which has to be mentioned separately.
- It does not give any indication regarding the release or absorption of heat. This is mentioned separately.
- The reversibility of some of the reactions can be mentioned with a double-sided arrow.

Revision Zone

Balance the given chemical equations.

1. ______ Hg + ______ O_2 $\longrightarrow$ ______ HgO
2. ______ Al + ______ Cl_2 $\longrightarrow$ ______ $AlCl_3$
3. ______ Na + ______ O_2 $\longrightarrow$ ______ Na_2O

Keywords

Chemical reaction: a chemical change resulting in the formation of one or more new substances

Chemical equation: the representation of a chemical reaction using symbols and formulae

Molecular mass: the total average atomic mass of all the atoms of a molecule

In a Nutshell

- An atom is the smallest unit of matter.
- Chemical symbols are abbreviations used to denote elements.
- The symbolic representation of the composition of a chemical compound is known as its chemical formula.
- A chemical change occurs when two or more substances react to form new products that have an entirely different set of properties.

Exercise

1 Choose the correct answer for each of the following.

a. The symbol of silver is

i. Hb ii. Sb

iii. Ag iv. S

b. Identify the chemical formula of calcium hydroxide.

i. CaOH ii. $Ca(OH)_2$

iii. Ca_2OH iv. $(Ca)_2OH$

c. Identify the correct balanced chemical equation from the following equations.

i. $2BaCl_2 + Al_2(SO_4)_3 \longrightarrow 2BaSO_4 + AlCl_3$

ii. $3BaCl_2 + 2Al_2(SO_4)_3 \longrightarrow 3BaSO_4 + AlCl_3$

iii. $3BaCl_2 + Al_2(SO_4)_3 \longrightarrow 3BaSO_4 + 2AlCl_3$

iv. $BaCl_2 + Al_2(SO_4)_3 \longrightarrow BaSO_4 + 2AlCl_3$

d. Which of these is the correct molecular mass of $CaCO_3$?

i. 100 a.m.u ii. 200 a.m.u

iii. 300 a.m.u iv. 400 a.m.u

e. According to the law of conservation of mass ____________.

i. Mass of reactants = Mass of products

ii. Number of reactants = Number of products

iii. Mass of reactants > Mass of products

iv. Mass of reactants < Mass of products

2 Fill in the blanks.

a. A substance that contains only one kind of atoms is called __________ (an element/a mixture).

b. The Latin name of sodium is__________ (*kalium/natrium*).

c. The chemical symbol of platinum is__________ (P/Pt).

d. CaO is the chemical formula for ____________ (copper oxide / calcium oxide).

e. The ____________ (physical/chemical) state of the reactants and products are mentioned along with the conditions required for the chemical reaction.

3 Write T for True and F for False.

a. The number of atoms of each element remains the same before and after a chemical reaction.

b. The chemical formula represents one molecule of the compound.

c. The chemical symbol of Platinum is P.

d. The Latin name of potassium is kalium.

e. The name of copper and its symbol come from the Greek name Cuprum.

4 Define the following terms.

a. Element

b. Compound

c. Chemical symbol

d. Chemical formula

c. Molecular mass

5 Differentiate between the following.

a. Elements and compounds

b. Chemical reaction and chemical equation

c. Reactants and products

6 Choose the odd one out. Give reasons for the choice.

a. Fe, Hg, Cu, Ar

b. Hydrogen, methane, nitrogen, oxygen

c. Cu, MgO, Al, He

7 Answer the following questions in brief.

a. What is an element? Give any two characteristics.

b. Write the characteristics of chemical changes.

c. Calculate the molecular mass of $MgCO^3$.

d. What is the law of conservation of mass?

e. What is the difference between an element and a compound?

8 Answer the following questions in detail.

a. What are the steps involved in balancing a chemical equation? Explain with examples.

b. Calculate the amount of oxygen gas and potassium chloride formed during the decomposition of 49 g of potassium chlorate. (Atomic mass of potassium = 39; oxygen = 16 and chlorine = 35.4)

c. Calculate the amount of calcium sulphate obtained by dissolving 112 g of calcium oxide (quick lime) in dilute sulphuric acid. (Atomic mass of calcium = 40; carbon = 12; hydrogen = 1; oxygen = 16 and sulphur = 32.1).

d. Calculate the mass of potassium nitrate obtained by neutralizing a solution containing 28 g of potassium hydroxide with nitric acid. (Atomic mass of nitrogen = 14; potassium = 39; oxygen = 16 and hydrogen = 1).

e. Explain how elements got their symbols.

f. Write the features of the modern method of representing elements.

g. What are the steps involved in writing the chemical formula of magnesium chloride?

h. Following are the chemical formulae of some compounds. List the elements present and the number of atoms in each compound.

i. $CaCO_3$ ii. KNO_3

iii. H_2SO_4 iv. NaOH

9 Think and answer.

An element A has valency 1 and an element B has valency 3. What would be the formula of the compound formed by A and B if B is a metal?

10 Project

Take some chart papers and make game cards of various symbols, element names and valencies. Try to match the element cards with the relevant symbols and valencies.

11 In the Library

Collect information on the characteristics of a chemical reaction by referring to library books.

Worksheet

Subject Integration

Answer the following.

a. Zinc granules react with dilute hydrochloric acid to form zinc chloride and hydrogen gas.

   i. Write a balanced chemical equation for the above mentioned reaction.

   ____

   ii. Calculate the amount of zinc chloride obtained by dissolving 110 g of zinc granules in dilute hydrochloric acid.
   (Atomic mass of zinc = 65.39; atomic mass of hydrogen = 1 and atomic mass of chloride = 35.4)

   ____

b. The neutralization reaction of sodium hydroxide with sulphuric acid forms sodium sulphate salt and water.

   i. Write a balanced chemical equation for the above mentioned reaction.

   ____

   ii. Calculate the amount of sodium sulphate formed when a solution containing 100 g of sodium hydroxide reacts with sulphuric acid.
   (Atomic mass of sodium = 23; atomic mass of oxygen = 16, atomic mass of hydrogen = 1, atomic mass of sulphur = 32)

   ____

c. Depict the molecular arrangement of the state of matter of the products formed in the following chemical reactions.

1. $Fe + CuSO_4 \longrightarrow FeSO_4 + Cu$
2. $CaCO_3 \longrightarrow CaO + CO_2$
3. $NaOH + HCl \longrightarrow NaCl + H_2O$

Chemical Reactions

6

What I shall learn

- Types of chemical reactions
- Reactivity series
- Oxides
- Classification of oxides

Introduction

A chemical change in which one or more substances react or combine together resulting in the formation of one or more new substances is called a **chemical reaction**. In a chemical reaction, atoms or group of atoms of the original substance(s) basically rearrange themselves to form new substances.

In this rearrangement process, either two or more substances combine with each other to form new substances or a substance may separate into two or more new substances. In other words, a chemical reaction is a process in which chemical bonds between the combining substances are broken down and new bonds are formed by rearranging atoms in order to produce new substances.

During the course of a chemical reaction, change of energy occurs. Here, energy is either absorbed or released in the form of heat and light. In few cases, sound is also produced.

Some real-life examples where energy is released or absorbed are as follows.

- When a fuel is burned, it releases a lot of energy in the form of heat. Fuels like petrol, diesel and kerosene are mainly made of methane. These burn to form carbon dioxide and release heat energy.

$$\underset{\text{Methane}}{CH_4} + \underset{\text{Oxygen}}{2O_2} \longrightarrow \underset{\text{Carbon dioxide}}{CO_2} + \underset{\text{Water}}{2H_2O} + \text{Heat}$$

- During photosynthesis, energy from sunlight is absorbed by plants and used in preparing food.

$$\underset{\text{Carbon dioxide}}{6CO_2} + \underset{\text{Water}}{12H_2O} \xrightarrow[\text{Sunlight (light energy)}]{\text{chlorophyll}} \underset{\text{Glucose}}{C_6H_{12}O_6} + \underset{\text{Oxygen}}{6O_2} + \underset{\text{Water}}{6H_2O}$$

- Bursting of crackers release a lot of energy in the form of heat.
- During cooking of food, heat energy is absorbed.

Do You Know?

The chemical reactions in which the reactants and products obtained have the same physical state are called **homogeneous reactions**.

The chemical reactions in which the reactants and products obtained do not have the same physical state are called **heterogeneous reactions**.

Activity 1

Aim: To observe that during chemical reactions new substances are formed

Materials required: Magnesium ribbon, Bunsen burner, tongs and china dish

Procedure:

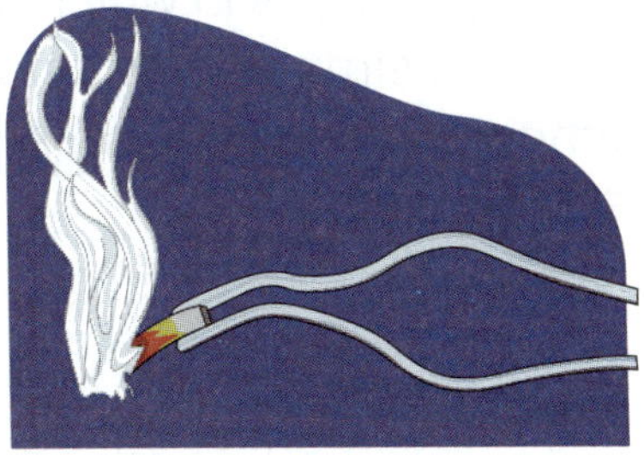

Burning of magnesium ribbon

1. Take a clean piece of magnesium ribbon (8-10 cm long).
2. With the help of tongs, heat the magnesium ribbon over the Bunsen burner flame.
3. You will observe that magnesium burns with a dazzling white light and forms white-coloured powder (magnesium oxide).
4. Collect the powder in the china dish.

Conclusion: We can observe that magnesium burns in the presence of oxygen to form magnesium oxide. Here, magnesium oxide is a new compound and it is formed by the combination of magnesium and oxygen.

Types of Chemical Reactions

Depending upon the nature of chemical changes happening, chemical reactions can be categorized into the following types.

Combination Reactions

Chemical reactions in which two or more reactants (elements or compounds) combine to form a single product are known as **combination reactions**. Combination reactions are also called **synthesis reactions**. A combination or synthesis reaction can be represented by the following general equation:

$$\mathbf{A + Y \longrightarrow AY}$$

- Calcium oxide (lime) reacts with water to form slaked lime or calcium hydroxide.

$$\underset{\text{Calcium oxide}}{CaO} + \underset{\text{Water}}{H_2O} \longrightarrow \underset{\text{Calcium hydroxide}}{Ca(OH)_2}$$

- Carbon burns in the presence of oxygen to form carbon dioxide gas.

$$\underset{\text{Carbon}}{C} + \underset{\text{Oxygen}}{O_2} \xrightarrow{\text{heat}} \underset{\text{Carbon dioxide}}{CO_2(g)}$$

- Calcium hydroxide reacts with carbon dioxide to form calcium carbonate and water.

$$\underset{\text{Calcium hydroxide}}{Ca(OH)_2} + \underset{\text{Carbon dioxide}}{CO_2} \longrightarrow \underset{\text{Calcium carbonate}}{CaCO_3(s)} + \underset{\text{Water}}{H_2O}$$

Decomposition Reactions

Chemical reactions in which a single reactant (compound) splits or breaks down to give two or more simpler products (constituent elements or other compounds) are known as **decomposition reactions**. A decomposition reaction can be represented by the following general equation:

$$AY \longrightarrow A + Y$$

For decomposition reactions to occur, energy in the form of electricity, heat, light, etc., is required.

When lead (IV) oxide is heated, it splits to form lead (II) oxide and oxygen.

$$\underset{\text{Lead (IV) oxide}}{2PbO_2} \xrightarrow{\text{heat}} \underset{\text{Lead (II) oxide}}{2PbO} + \underset{\text{Oxygen}}{O_2}$$

- Decomposition reactions that require energy in the form of heat are known as **thermal decomposition reactions**. These reactions are also known as thermolysis (thermo means 'heat' and lysis means 'breaking'). For example:

  Calcium carbonate on heating decomposes into calcium oxide and carbon dioxide.

$$\underset{\text{Calcium carbonate}}{CaCO_3\,(s)} \xrightarrow{\text{heat}} \underset{\text{Calcium Oxide}}{CaO\,(s)} + \underset{\text{Carbon Dioxide}}{CO_2\,(g)}$$

- Decomposition reactions that require energy in the form of light are known as **photochemical** or **photolytic decomposition reactions**. These reactions are also known as photolysis (*photo* means 'light' and *lysis* means 'breaking'). For example:

  Silver chloride, in the presence of light, decomposes into silver and chlorine.

$$\underset{\text{Silver chloride}}{2AgCl} \xrightarrow{\text{light}} \underset{\text{Silver}}{2Ag\,(s)} + \underset{\text{Chlorine}}{Cl_2\,(g)}$$

- Decomposition reactions that require energy in the form of electricity are known as **electrolytic decomposition reactions**. These reactions are also known as **electrolysis**. For example:

  When electric current is passed through water, it decomposes into hydrogen and oxygen.

$$\underset{\text{Water}}{2H_2O\,(l)} \xrightarrow{\text{electric current}} \underset{\text{Hydrogen}}{2H_2\,(g)} + \underset{\text{Oxygen}}{O_2\,(g)}$$

Simple Displacement Reactions

Chemical reactions in which one element replaces or displaces the other element from its compound and forms a new compound are known as **displacement reactions**. These reactions are also known as **substitution reactions**.

Usually, the more reactive element (metal or non-metal) replaces the less reactive element (metal or non-metal) from its solution. A displacement reaction can be represented by the following general equation.

$$\mathbf{A + BY \longrightarrow AY + B}$$

Examples of displacement reactions are as follows.

- Zinc reacts with copper sulphate solution to form zinc sulphate and copper.

$$\underset{\text{Zinc}}{Zn\,(s)} + \underset{\text{Copper sulphate}}{CuSO_4\,(aq)} \longrightarrow \underset{\text{Zinc sulphate}}{ZnSO_4\,(aq)} + \underset{\text{Copper}}{Cu\,(s)}$$

  Zinc is more reactive than copper. So, it displaces copper from its salt solution. The reverse reaction will not take place as copper is less reactive than zinc.

$$\underset{\text{Copper}}{Cu} + \underset{\text{Zinc sulphate}}{ZnSO_4} \longrightarrow \text{no reaction}$$

- Sodium reacts with hydrochloric acid to form sodium chloride and hydrogen gas. Sodium is more reactive than hydrogen and thus it displaces hydrogen from hydrochloric acid.

$$\underset{\text{Sodium}}{2Na\,(s)} + \underset{\text{Hydrochloric acid}}{2HCl\,(aq)} \longrightarrow \underset{\text{Sodium chloride}}{2NaCl\,(aq)} + \underset{\text{Hydrogen}}{H_2\,(g)}$$

Double Displacement Reactions

Chemical reactions in which an exchange of ions takes place between two reactants (compounds in their aqueous solution) to form new compounds are called **double displacement reactions**. These reactions are also known as double decomposition reactions. A double displacement reaction can be represented by the following general equation.

$$\mathbf{AB + XY \longrightarrow AY + XB}$$

A double displacement reaction is of two types: precipitation reaction and neutralization reaction.

1. **Precipitation Reaction**: A type of double displacement reaction in which two compounds in their aqueous solutions react to form an insoluble solid (called precipitate) as one of the products is known as a **precipitation reaction**. For example:

   - When potassium sulphate solution reacts with barium chloride solution, barium sulphate (an insoluble white precipitate) and potassium chloride are formed.

$$\underset{\text{Potassium sulphate}}{K_2SO_4\,(aq)} + \underset{\text{Barium chloride}}{BaCl_2\,(aq)} \longrightarrow \underset{\text{Potassium chloride}}{2KCl\,(aq)} + \underset{\text{Barium sulphate}}{BaSO_4\,(s)\downarrow}$$

   - When sodium chloride solution reacts with silver nitrate solution, silver chloride (an insoluble white precipitate) and sodium nitrate are formed.

$$\underset{\text{Sodium chloride}}{NaCl\,(aq)} + \underset{\text{Silver nitrate}}{AgNO_3\,(aq)} \longrightarrow \underset{\text{Sodium nitrate}}{NaNO_3\,(aq)} + \underset{\text{Silver chloride}}{AgCl\,(s)\downarrow}$$

2. **Neutralization Reaction:** A type of double displacement reaction in which an acid reacts with a base resulting in the formation of salt and water is called a **neutralization reaction**. The salt formed contains the cation from the base and the anion from the acid. The hydrogen ion (H^+) of the acid combines with the hydroxyl ion (OH^-) of the base to form water. For example:
   - When sodium hydroxide solution (base) reacts with dilute hydrochloric acid, sodium chloride (salt) and water are formed.

$$\underset{\text{Sodium hydroxide}}{NaOH\,(aq)} + \underset{\text{Hydrochloric acid}}{HCl\,(aq)} \longrightarrow \underset{\text{Sodium chloride}}{NaCl\,(aq)} + \underset{\text{Water}}{H_2O}$$

   - When zinc oxide (base) reacts with nitric acid, zinc nitrate (salt) and water are formed.

$$\underset{\text{zinc Oxide}}{ZnO} + \underset{\text{Nitric acid}}{2HNO_3} \longrightarrow \underset{\text{Zinc nitrate}}{Zn(NO_3)_2} + \underset{\text{Water}}{H_2O}$$

Revision Zone

Match the following.

Column 1	**Column 2**
$A + Y \longrightarrow AY$	Displacement reaction
$AB + XY \longrightarrow AY + XB$	Decomposition reaction
$AY \longrightarrow A + Y$	Double displacement reaction
$A + BY \longrightarrow AY + B$	Combination reaction

Reactivity Series

Potassium	K	Most reactive
Sodium	Na	↓
Calcium	Ca	
Magnesium	Mg	
Aluminium	Al	
Zinc	Zn	
Iron	Fe	
Tin	Sn	
Lead	Pb	
Hydrogen	H	
Copper	Cu	
Mercury	Hg	
Silver	Ag	
Gold	Au	
Platinum	Pt	Least reactive

▲ Reactivity series of metals

The arrangement of metals in the decreasing order of their reactivity is called the **reactivity series** of metals. The metals placed higher in the reactivity series are more reactive than those placed below them.

Being a non-metal, hydrogen is also placed in the reactivity series because just like metals, it can also lose one electron and attain a positive charge (H^+) during chemical reactions.

A more reactive metal can displace a less reactive metal from its salt solution, that is, if the former metal is placed at a higher position in the reactivity series than the metal present in the salt solution.

However, a less reactive metal that is placed at a lower position in the reactivity series cannot displace a more reactive metal present in the salt solution.

Example: Iron reacts with copper sulphate to form iron sulphate and copper.

$$Fe + CuSO_4 \longrightarrow FeSO_4 + Cu$$

Iron is more reactive than copper because it is placed higher than copper in the reactivity series. So, it can displace copper from its salt solution. The reverse reaction will not take place as copper is less reactive than iron.

$$Cu + FeSO_4 \longrightarrow \text{no reaction}$$

You can see the positions of copper and iron in the reactivity series. Thus, the reactivity series indicates which metals are more reactive as compared to others. Also, by looking at the reactivity series, we can predict whether a displacement reaction will take place or not.

Activity 2

Note: *This activity needs to be performed carefully in the presence and with the assistance of a teacher.*

Aim: To examine that a more reactive metal can displace a less reactive metal from its salt solution

Materials required: Three 250 ml glass beakers, 100 ml of copper sulphate solution, 100 ml of silver nitrate solution, 100 ml of iron sulphate solution, a small piece of zinc metal and two small pieces of copper turnings

Procedure:

Take three clean 250 ml glass beakers and label them as samples 1, 2 and 3. Take about 100 ml of copper sulphate solution in beaker 1, 100 ml of silver nitrate solution in beaker 2 and 100 ml of iron sulphate solution in beaker 3. Add a small piece of zinc metal to beaker 1. Add small pieces of copper turnings to beakers 2 and 3. Keep the beakers undisturbed for a few minutes and record your observations.

Observation:

S. No.	Samples	Observation
1.	Sample 1 (Copper sulphate + Zinc)	The solution becomes colourless and copper is displaced
2.	Sample 2 (Silver nitrate + Copper)	Silver is displaced and deposits on copper turnings
3.	Sample 3 (Iron sulphate + Copper)	No reaction

Conclusion: A more reactive metal can displace a less reactive metal from its salt solution.

Endothermic and Exothermic Reactions

Chemical reactions generally involve a change of energy during the course of the reaction. Energy is either absorbed or liberated during a chemical reaction and it is mostly in the form of heat and light. In some cases, sound is also produced. Based on whether heat energy is absorbed or liberated, chemical reactions are of two types.

Find Out

Arrange the following metals in increasing order of their reactivity.

Copper, Silver, Aluminium, Magnesium, Iron

i. **Exothermic reactions**: Chemical reactions in which heat energy is liberated are called **exothermic reactions**. For example, when carbon burns in the presence of oxygen, carbon dioxide is formed along with the generation of heat.

$$\underset{\text{Carbon}}{C} + \underset{\text{Oxygen}}{O_2} \longrightarrow \underset{\text{Carbon dioxide}}{CO_2} + \text{Heat}$$

Other examples of exothermic reactions are respiration, burning of fuels like coal, petrol and kerosene, and rusting.

ii. **Endothermic reactions**: Chemical reactions in which heat energy is absorbed from the surroundings are called **endothermic reactions**. For example, when carbon and sulphur are heated together, carbon disulphide is formed.

$$\underset{\text{Carbon}}{C} + \underset{\text{Sulphur}}{2S} + \text{Heat} \longrightarrow \underset{\text{Carbon disulphide}}{CS_2}$$

When calcium carbonate is heated to a high temperature, calcium oxide and carbon dioxide are produced.

$$\underset{\text{Calcium carbonate}}{CaCO_3} \xrightarrow{\text{Heat}} \underset{\text{Calcium oxide}}{CaO} + \underset{\text{Carbon dioxide}}{CO_2}$$

Do You Know?

When we apply nail polish remover, we get a cooling effect on our finger nails and toe nails. This is because the acetone present in the nail polish remover absorbs heat from our body while evaporating.

Activity 3

Note: *This activity needs to be demonstrated by the teacher.*

Aim: To infer that the reaction of an acid with a base is an exothermic reaction

Materials required: Beaker, 10 ml concentrated hydrochloric acid, 10 ml sodium hydroxide solution, thermometer, droppers and glass rod

Procedure:

1. Take a clean beaker and add 10 ml of concentrated hydrochloric acid using a clean dropper.
2. With a fresh dropper, gradually add sodium hydroxide solution.
3. Stir the solution with the help of a glass rod.
4. Place the thermometer in the solution and observe the reading.

Observation: When the thermometer is placed in the solution, a rise in temperature is noted.

Conclusion: During the reaction of an acid with a base, a large amount of energy is released. This results in an increase in temperature. Hence, this reaction is an exothermic reaction.

Activity 4

Note: *This activity needs to be demonstrated by the teacher.*

Aim: To infer that dissolution of ammonium chloride in water is an endothermic reaction

Materials required: Beaker, ammonium chloride, 50 ml distilled water, spatula and glass rod

Procedure:

1. Take a clean beaker and add 50 ml distilled water.
2. With the help of a spatula, add ammonium chloride to the water.
3. Stir the solution with the help of a glass rod.
4. Place the thermometer in the solution and observe the reading.

Observation: When the thermometer is placed in the solution, a decrease in temperature is noted.

Conclusion: During dissolution of ammonium chloride, energy is absorbed. This results in a decrease in temperature. Hence, dissolution of ammonium chloride is an endothermic reaction.

Oxides

Decomposition reactions to form oxides: Decomposition is a chemical reaction where reactants split or break down to form simpler products. When compounds such as metal carbonates, nitrates and sulphates are heated to high temperature, they decompose to form respective metal oxides. Some of the examples are as follows.

- When a metal carbonate is heated, it decomposes to form respective metal oxide and carbon dioxide.

$$\underset{\text{Calcium carbonate}}{CaCO_3\,(s)} \xrightarrow{\text{heat}} \underset{\text{Calcium oxide}}{CaO\,(s)} + \underset{\text{Carbon dioxide}}{CO_2\,(g)}$$

- When a metal nitrate is heated, it decomposes to form respective metal oxide, nitrogen dioxide and oxygen.

$$\underset{\text{Magnesium nitrate}}{2Mg\,(NO_3)_2} \xrightarrow{\text{heat}} \underset{\text{Magnesium oxide}}{2MgO} \quad \underset{\text{Nitrogen dioxide}}{4NO_2} + \underset{\text{Oxygen}}{O_2}$$

- When a metal sulphate is heated, it decomposes to form respective metal oxide, sulphur dioxide and sulphur trioxide.

$$\underset{\text{Iron sulphate}}{2FeSO_4} \xrightarrow{\text{heat}} \underset{\text{Iron oxide}}{Fe_2O_3} + \underset{\text{Sulphur dioxide}}{SO_2} + \underset{\text{Sulphur trioxide}}{SO_3}$$

Activity 5

Note: *This activity needs to be performed carefully in the presence and with the assistance of a teacher.*

Aim: To infer heating of calcium carbonate yields calcium oxide

Materials required: Bunsen burner, calcium carbonate (limestone), wire gauze, tripod stand

Procedure:

1. Take a few lumps of limestone.
2. Place the lumps on wire gauze. Keep the gauze on a tripod stand and heat with a roaring Bunsen burner flame for 15 min.
3. If the room is dark, then glowing of lumps can be seen.

Observation: Calcium carbonate splits to form calcium oxide and carbon dioxide.

Equation: $$CaCO_3 \xrightarrow{\text{Heat}} CaO + CO_2$$

Note: As calcium carbonate and calcium oxide are white in colour, one cannot distinguish the formation of calcium oxide.

Activity 6

Note: *This activity needs to be performed carefully in the presence and with the assistance of a teacher.*

Aim: To infer heating of lead carbonate yields lead oxide

Materials required: Bunsen burner, test tube, test tube holder and lead carbonate

Procedure:

1. Take about 2 spatulas full of lead carbonate in a test tube.
2. Hold the test tube with a holder and heat over Bunsen burner flame.

Observation: Lead carbonate which is white in colour decomposes to lead oxide (yellow colour) and carbon dioxide is released.

Equation: $$PbCO_3 \xrightarrow{\text{Heat}} PbO + CO_2$$

Classification of Oxides

Oxides are compounds that are formed by the reaction of oxygen with other elements. Oxygen reacts with both metals and non-metals to form respective oxides. Oxygen is highly reactive in nature.

Based on the nature and the properties exhibited by compounds, oxides are classified into four main groups:

1. Acidic oxides: Non-metals react with oxygen to form acidic compounds of oxygen, also called acid anhydrides or acidic oxides, and when these combine with bases, salts are formed. The acidic oxides can be tested with litmus paper (these oxides turn a blue litmus paper to red). Examples: CO_2, SO_3, SO_2 etc.

$$\underset{\text{Sulphur trioxide}}{SO_3} + \underset{\text{Water}}{H_2O} \longrightarrow \underset{\text{Sulphuric acid}}{H_2SO_4}$$

$$\underset{\text{Sulphur dioxide}}{SO_2} + \underset{\text{Sodium hydroxide}}{2NaOH} \longrightarrow \underset{\text{Sodium sulphite (salt)}}{Na_2SO_3} + \underset{\text{Water}}{H_2O}$$

2. Basic oxides: Metals react with oxygen to give basic compounds of oxygen, also called base anhydrides or basic oxides, and when these combine with acids, salts are formed. The basic oxides can be tested with litmus paper (these oxides turn a red litmus paper to blue). Examples: CaO, MgO, Na_2O, K_2O etc.

$$\underset{\text{Sodium oxide}}{Na_2O} + \underset{\text{Water}}{H_2O} \longrightarrow \underset{\text{Sodium hydroxide}}{2NaOH}$$

$$\underset{\text{Sodium oxide}}{Na_2O} + \underset{\text{Sulphuric acid}}{H_2SO_4} \longrightarrow \underset{\text{Sodium sulphate (salt)}}{Na_2SO_4} + \underset{\text{Water}}{H_2O}$$

3. Amphoteric oxides: These are compounds of oxygen which exhibit both acidic and basic characteristics. These oxides on reaction with acid undergo neutralization reaction to form water and salt, thus exhibiting the basic property of the compound. Similarly, on reaction with base, they form salt and water, thus exhibiting the acidic property of the compound. Amphoteric oxides do not show any colour change neither with blue litmus nor with red litmus paper. Examples: Al_2O_3, ZnO, PbO, SnO etc.

$$\underset{\text{Zinc oxide}}{ZnO} + \underset{\text{Hydrochloric acid}}{2HCl} \longrightarrow \underset{\text{Zinc chloride}}{ZnCl_2} + \underset{\text{Water}}{H_2O} \quad \text{(basic nature)}$$

$$\underset{\text{Zinc oxide}}{ZnO} + \underset{\text{Sodium hydroxide}}{2NaOH} \longrightarrow \underset{\text{Zincate sodium}}{Na_2ZnO_2} + \underset{\text{Water}}{H_2O} \quad \text{(acidic nature)}$$

4. Neutral oxides: Some compounds on reaction with oxygen form oxides which neither exhibit acidic nor basic characteristics. And hence they do not form salts on reaction with acids or bases. Such compounds are called neutral compounds of oxygen. Examples: NO, CO, N_2O etc.

Activity 7

Aim: To test whether the given oxide is acidic, basic or neutral

Materials required: Test tube, glass rod, magnesium oxide (MgO), litmus paper and water

Procedure:

1. Take a test tube and add water to it.
2. Add magnesium oxide to the test tube and stir with a glass rod.
3. Test the solution with a litmus paper and record your observation.

Observation and Conclusion:

Sample	Colour change	Conclusion
Magnesium oxide + water	Red litmus paper turns to blue	Magnesium oxide is a basic oxide.

Revision Zone

Write T for True or F for False.

1. Decomposition of calcium carbonate is an example of endothermic reaction.
2. When metal sulphates are heated at high temperature, it yields metal oxide, sulphur dioxide and sulphur trioxide.
3. Copper cannot displace iron from iron sulphate solution.
4. Zinc oxide exhibits both acidic and basic properties.
5. Carbon monoxide is an example of amphoteric oxide.

Keywords

Chemical reaction: a chemical change resulting in the formation of one or more new substances

Combination reactions: chemical reactions in which two or more reactants (elements or compounds) combine to form a single product

Decomposition reactions: chemical reactions in which a single reactant splits or breaks down to give two or more products

Exothermic reactions: chemical reactions in which heat is evolved

Endothermic reactions: chemical reactions in which heat is absorbed

Double displacement reactions: chemical reactions in which an exchange of ions takes place between two reactants (aqueous solution) to form new compounds

Reactivity series: the arrangement of metals in the decreasing order of their reactivity

Neutralization reaction: a type of chemical reaction in which an acid reacts with a base to form salt and water

In a Nutshell

- Chemical reactions are of four types: combination reaction, decomposition reaction, displacement reaction and double displacement reaction.
- In reactivity series, metals are arranged in the decreasing order of their reactivity.
- In an endothermic reaction, energy is absorbed, while in an exothermic reaction, energy is liberated.
- Oxides are of four types: acidic oxides, basic oxides, amphoteric oxides and neutral oxides.

Exercise

1 Choose the correct answer for each of the following.

a. The following reaction is an example of _______.

$Fe_2O_3 + 2Al \longrightarrow Al_2O_3 + 2Fe$

i. combination reaction
ii. displacement reaction
iii. decomposition reaction
iv. double displacement reaction

b. The following reaction is an example of _________.

$NH_3 + HCl \longrightarrow NH_4Cl$

i. double displacement reaction
ii. displacement reaction
iii. combination reaction
iv. decomposition reaction

c. Which among the following is the most reactive metal?

i. Sodium
ii. Potassium
iii. Gold
iv. Silver

d. Which of the following is an example of endothermic reaction?

i. Burning of fuels
ii. Dissolution of ammonium chloride in water
iii. Rusting
iv. Respiration

e. Which of the following statements is true about basic oxides?

i. They form salts with bases.
ii. They turn blue litmus to red.
iii. Carbon dioxide is an example of basic oxide.
iv. They turn red litmus to blue.

2 Fill in the blanks.

a. The reaction in which heat energy is released is known as __________ (exothermic/endothermic) reaction.

b. A reaction in which a single substance splits to give two or more substances is called ______________(decomposition/displacement) reaction.

c. The oxides that exhibit both acidic and basic characteristics are called ____________. (neutral oxides/amphoteric oxides)

d. The decomposition reaction that occur in the presence of light is known as _________ (photolysis/thermolysis).

e. Displacement reactions are also called __________ reactions. (substitution/synthesis)

3 Write T for True and F for False

a. Precipitation reactions produce insoluble salts.

b. Reaction of sodium chloride solution with silver nitrate solution is an example of a decomposition reaction.

c. Al_2O_3 is an example of neutral oxide.

d. Magnesium oxide is obtained from the decomposition of magnesium sulphate.

e. The products of a neutralization reaction are salt and water.

4 Define the following terms.

a. Electrolysis
b. Neutralization reactions
c. Reactivity series
d. Amphoteric oxides
e. Endothermic reactions

5. **Identify the type of chemical reaction.**

   a. $Fe + CuSO_4 \longrightarrow FeSO_4 + Cu$
   b. $2Na + Cl_2 \longrightarrow 2NaCl$
   c. $CaCO_3 \longrightarrow CaO + CO_2$
   d. $BaCl_2 + Na_2SO_4 \longrightarrow BaSO_4 + 2NaCl$

6. **Answer the following questions in brief.**

   a. Distinguish between exothermic and endothermic reactions.
   b. Write a short note on decomposition reaction and its types.
   c. List the properties of amphoteric oxides.
   d. Explain neutralization reaction with example.
   e. Explain the reaction of zinc with copper sulphate with the help of appropriate chemical equations.

7. **Answer the following questions in detail.**

   a. Explain the various types of chemical reactions with an example for each.
   b. Explain the arrangement of metals in the reactivity series in detail.
   c. Explain the formation of oxides from decomposition of metal carbonates, nitrates and sulphates.
   d. What are the different types of oxides? Explain with examples.
   e. Explain endothermic and exothermic reactions with examples.

8. **Think and answer.**

   Sample A can displace sample B from its salt solution and sample B can displace sample C, but sample C cannot displace samples A and B. Samples A and B are placed below calcium and above hydrogen in the reactivity series, whereas sample C is the least reactive metal and is situated in between mercury and gold.

   Mention the names of these samples and arrange them in the decreasing order of their reactivity.

9. **In the Laboratory**

   Preform an activity to test whether nitric oxide and sulphur dioxide are acidic, basic, amphoteric or neutral oxides.

10. **In the Library**

    Refer library books and collect information on real-life applications of exothermic and endothermic reactions.

Worksheet

❶ **Life Skills**

Names of different oxides are given in the following table. Mention the colour change that these oxides show with a red or blue litmus paper. Also, identify the nature of the type of oxide and record it in the table given below.

Type of oxide	Colour change with blue or red litmus paper	Conclusion
Sulphur dioxide		
Calcium oxide		
Lead oxide		
Carbon monoxide		
Nitric oxide		
Zinc oxide		
Potassium oxide		
Sulphur trioxide		

❷ Illustrate how metals are arranged in the reactivity series based on their reactivity in the space given below.

Hydrogen

7

What I shall learn

- Occurrence of hydrogen
- Preparation of hydrogen
- Properties of hydrogen
- Uses of hydrogen

Introduction

We have learned in the previous classes that hydrogen gas puts off a burning splinter with a 'pop' sound.

In 1766, British scientist Henry Cavendish discovered hydrogen by adding zinc to dilute sulphuric acid. He initially named the gas as 'inflammable air'. In 1783, French scientist Antoine Lavoisier named the gas as 'hydrogen'.

The word hydrogen comes from the Greek words *hydro* meaning 'water' and *genes* meaning 'formed' based on the finding that water is produced when hydrogen is burned.

Let us learn in detail about the occurrence, properties and uses of hydrogen in this chapter.

▲ Hydrogen exists in the Sun in huge amounts

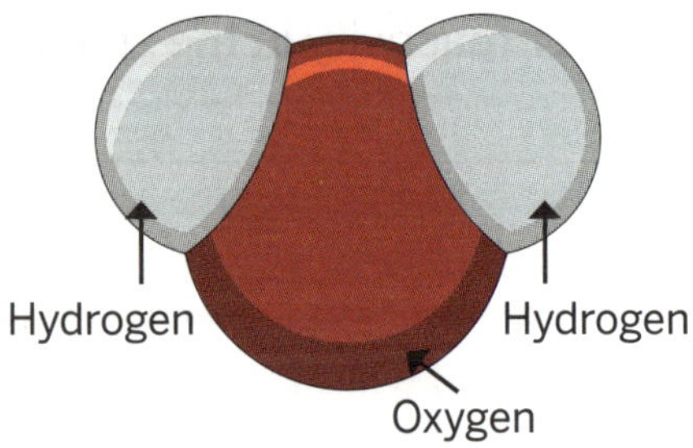

▲ Molecular structure of water (a combined form of hydrogen)

Occurrence of Hydrogen

Hydrogen is one of the most abundant elements on Earth. The free form of hydrogen exists in the Sun, stars and in volcanic gases. Due to nuclear reactions that involve hydrogen gas, a large amount of heat and light is released in the Sun and stars.

Hydrogen occurs abundantly on Earth in the combined form as compounds like water, hydrocarbons, acids and oils. It occurs as a constituent in animal and plant tissues in the form of proteins, fats and carbohydrates.

Preparation of Hydrogen

Let us look at the methods to prepare hydrogen.

Preparation of Hydrogen from Water by Electrolysis

Hydrogen is prepared by passing electric current through water that contains a small quantity of acid, such as, dilute sulphuric acid. This method is called **electrolysis of water** and is widely used in the industrial preparation of hydrogen.

$$2H_2O \xrightarrow{\text{Electric current}} 2H_2\uparrow + O_2\uparrow$$

Water → Hydrogen + Oxygen

The process of passing electric current through a chemical substance or compound in its aqueous solution or molten state to bring about a chemical change is known as **electrolysis**.

Challenge Yourself

Why is a small quantity of dilute H2SO4 added to water for electrolysis?

In an electrolysis set-up, the important components are electrolytic cell, electrolyte, electrodes and battery.

1. **Electrolytic cell**: The process of electrolysis takes place in a container called the electrolytic cell. It is a device that converts electrical energy into chemical energy or vice versa. It contains electrodes dipped in the electrolyte.
2. **Electrolyte**: Electrolyte is the molten or aqueous solution of a chemical compound through which current passes to carry out the chemical reaction. In the solution or molten state, the compounds dissociate into ions. The oppositely charged ions flow towards their respective electrodes, which causes the flow of current.
3. **Electrodes**: Electrodes are the two conducting terminals or rods dipped in the electrolyte solution. Electric current enters or leaves an electrolyte through these conducting rods. Electrodes are made up of metals or graphite.

   The electrode that is connected to the positive terminal of the battery is called the **anode** (positive electrode) and the electrode that is connected to the negative terminal of the battery is called the **cathode** (negative electrode).
4. **Battery**: The electrodes are connected to a battery which provides electric current.

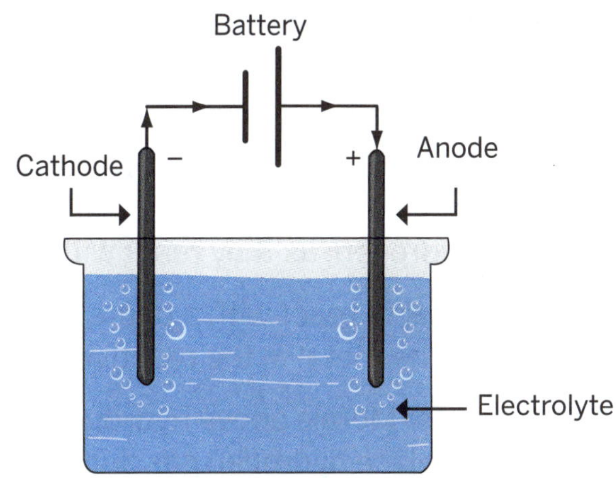

▲ Set-up for electrolysis

When electric current is passed through the electrodes of an electrolytic cell, the ions in the electrolyte move towards the oppositely charged electrodes. Cations (positive charges) move towards the cathode, whereas anions (negative charges) move towards the anode

Science In Context

The arrangement of metals in the decreasing order of their reactivity is called the **reactivity series** of metals.

Inspite of being a non-metal, hydrogen is also placed in the reactivity series because just like metals it can lose one electron and attain a positive charge (H^+) during chemical reactions.

Metal	Symbol	Reactivity
Potassium	K	Most reactive
Sodium	Na	
Calcium	Ca	
Magnesium	Mg	
Aluminium	Al	
Zinc	Zn	
Iron	Fe	
Tin	Sn	
Lead	Pb	
Hydrogen	H	
Copper	Cu	
Mercury	Hg	
Silver	Ag	
Gold	Au	
Platinum	Pt	Least reactive

(Decreasing order of reactivity ↓)

Science in Context

The hydrogen gas produced in chemical reactions can be tested by bringing a lighted matchstick near it as the gas burns with a 'pop' sound.

Do You Know?

Hydrogen gas that is just formed after a chemical reaction is referred to as 'nascent hydrogen' or 'newly born hydrogen'.

of the electrolytic cell. This causes the constituents of the electrolyte to gradually get deposited on the electrodes.

Laboratory Preparation of Hydrogen

In the laboratory, hydrogen is prepared by the reaction of zinc granules with dilute hydrochloric acid or dilute sulphuric acid.

Zn	+	dil. $2HCl$	$\longrightarrow$	$ZnCl_2$	+	$H_2\uparrow$
Zinc		Dil. Hydrochloric Acid		Zinc Chloride		Hydrogen

Zn	+	dil. H_2SO_4	$\longrightarrow$	$ZnSO_4$	+	$H_2\uparrow$
Zinc		Dil. Sulphuric Acid		Zinc Sulphate		Hydrogen

In this process, zinc granules are preferred over pure zinc because pure zinc is non-porous and the reaction of pure zinc with the dilute acids (sulphuric acid; nitric acid) is very slow. Also, zinc is preferred to other metals because the reaction of zinc with either dilute HCl or dilute H_2SO_4 can be easily controlled in the laboratory.

Note: Metals like sodium (Na) and potassium (K) are not preferred for the preparation of hydrogen, though they produce hydrogen, as they react with mineral acids very violently.

For any metal to react with a dilute mineral acid for the synthesis of hydrogen depends on the position of the metal in the reactivity series.

For example: Metals above hydrogen (Ca, Mg, Zn, Na) in the reactivity series react with dilute acids to displace hydrogen gas and form their respective salts.

Metals like platinum, gold, silver and copper do not displace hydrogen either from acids or from water. This is because they are less reactive as compared to hydrogen and are placed below hydrogen in the reactivity series.

Dilute nitric acid (HNO_3), being a very strong oxidizing agent, will not liberate hydrogen with metals, instead it forms water. (Only when magnesium reacts with very dilute nitric acid, hydrogen is formed.)

Choice of dilute acids (other than dil. nitric acid) in preparation of hydrogen

An active metal usually displaces hydrogen gas. Dilute nitric acid (HNO_3) is a very strong oxidizing agent which can oxidize the free hydrogen and convert into water. On the other hand, the use of concentrated nitric acid results in the formation of a mixture of oxides of nitrogen. Therefore, dilute HNO_3 is not used for hydrogen preparation.

Other mineral acids like dilute hydrochloric acid and dilute sulphuric acid are extensively used in the preparation of hydrogen. However, concentrated sulphuric acid is not used in the preparation of hydrogen on reaction with zinc as it will produce sulphur dioxide (SO_2) instead of H_2 gas.

Activity 1

Aim: To prepare hydrogen gas in the laboratory using dilute hydrochloric acid and zinc granules

Materials required: Thistle funnel, dilute hydrochloric acid, delivery tube, two-holed rubber cork, zinc granules, Woulfe bottle, inverted gas jar, trough, water and beehive shelf

Note: This activity needs to be performed very carefully as a teacher demonstration.

Precautions:

- Make sure the entire set-up is airtight.
- The end of the thistle funnel must be dipped in the dilute hydrochloric acid solution.
- The entire set-up should be kept away from fire.
- The collection of hydrogen gas should be done only after the entire volume of air inside the apparatus is expelled out.

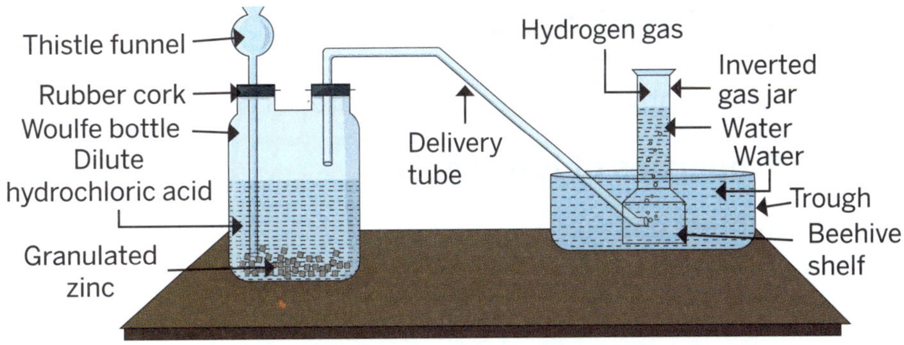

Procedure: Set up the apparatus as shown in the figure.

Take a few zinc granules in a Woulfe bottle and close it with a two-holed rubber cork. Fix the thistle funnel in one hole and the delivery tube in the other hole of the rubber cork. Connect the other end of the delivery tube to the beehive shelf that is immersed under the water in the trough. Gently pour the dilute hydrochloric acid through the thistle funnel until the zinc granules are completely immersed.

Observation: Formation of hydrogen gas is seen in the form of bubbles at the end of the delivery tube.

Collection of the gas: Allow some hydrogen gas to escape from the jar as it is mixed with the air within the apparatus. Place an inverted gas jar filled with water on the beehive shelf. Collect the hydrogen gas by the downward displacement of water. It is collected by the downward displacement of water as it is lighter than air. When the bubbles stop forming, it indicates that the reaction is complete. Remove the gas jar from the trough that is filled with colourless hydrogen gas and keep it in the inverted position. Similarly, several jars can be used to collect more amount of hydrogen gas.

Bosch's Process

Bosch's process is used for the preparation of hydrogen industrially.

During this process, steam is passed at a temperature of 1200°C over carbon (red-hot coke) producing hydrogen gas and carbon monoxide.

$$\underset{\text{Carbon}}{C} + \underset{\text{Steam}}{H_2O(g)} \longrightarrow \underset{\text{Carbon monoxide}}{CO} + \underset{\text{Hydrogen gas}}{H_2}$$

The excess steam in the reaction again reacts with the water gas (i.e., a mixture of CO and H_2)

at a temperature of nearly 450°C in the presence of catalysts (chromium oxide or iron oxide) resulting in the further formation of hydrogen gas and carbon dioxide.

$$(CO + H_2) \text{ Water gas} + H_2O(g) \longrightarrow CO_2 + 2H_2$$

The carbon dioxide produced during this reaction is further made to dissolve in cold water or caustic potash solution under pressure of about 20-25 atmosphere. The undissolved hydrogen can be removed.

Properties of Hydrogen

Let us look at the physical and chemical properties of hydrogen.

Physical Properties of Hydrogen

- It is the lightest gas.
- It is colourless, odourless and tasteless in nature.
- It can conduct heat better than other gases.
- It is insoluble in water.

True Fact

Hydrogen can burn itself (combustible gas) but does not support the process of combustion.

Chemical Properties of Hydrogen

Let us look at how hydrogen reacts with various substances.

Reaction with Oxygen

Hydrogen reacts with oxygen to produce a pale blue-coloured flame and produces water vapour and heat energy.

$$\underset{\text{Hydrogen}}{2H_2} + \underset{\text{Oxygen}}{O_2} \longrightarrow \underset{\text{Water}}{2H_2O} + \text{Heat}$$

As heat energy is released in this reaction, this reaction is a combustion reaction and also an exothermic reaction.

Reaction with Chlorine

In the presence of diffused sunlight, hydrogen reacts with chlorine to form hydrogen chloride.

$$\underset{\text{Hydrogen}}{H_2} + \underset{\text{Chlorine}}{Cl_2} \longrightarrow \underset{\text{Hydrogen Chloride}}{2HCl}$$

In the presence of direct sunlight, the reaction of hydrogen with chlorine takes place with an explosion.

Reaction with Nitrogen

Hydrogen reacts with nitrogen under specific conditions like high pressure (200 atm), high temperature (450°C), presence of a catalyst (iron) and a promoter (molybdenum) to form ammonia.

$$\underset{\text{Hydrogen}}{3H_2} + \underset{\text{Nitrogen}}{N_2} \longrightarrow \underset{\text{Ammonia}}{2NH_3}$$

The above reaction is referred to as **Haber's process**.

Reaction with Sulphur

Hydrogen reacts with boiling sulphur to form hydrogen sulphide.

$$\underset{\text{Hydrogen}}{H_2} + \underset{\text{Sulphur}}{S} \longrightarrow \underset{\text{Hydrogen sulphide}}{H_2S}$$

Reaction with Litmus

Hydrogen being neutral (neither acidic nor basic) does not change the colour of either blue litmus or red litmus.

Reaction with Metals

Hydrogen reacts with highly reactive metals at high temperatures to form respective metal hydrides.

$$\underset{\text{Hydrogen}}{H_2} + \underset{\text{Potassium}}{2K} \longrightarrow \underset{\text{Potassium hydride}}{2KH}$$

$$\underset{\text{Hydrogen}}{H_2} + \underset{\text{Sodium}}{2Na} \longrightarrow \underset{\text{Sodium hydride}}{2NaH}$$

$$\underset{\text{Hydrogen}}{H_2} + \underset{\text{Calcium}}{Ca} \longrightarrow \underset{\text{Calcium hydride}}{CaH_2}$$

Reducing Property of Hydrogen: Oxidation–reduction Reactions

Oxidation: The process of removal of hydrogen or addition of oxygen to a substance is known as **oxidation** and the substance that removes hydrogen or produces oxygen is called an **oxidizing agent**.

$$\underset{\text{Zinc}}{2Zn} + \underset{\substack{\text{Oxygen} \\ \text{(Oxidizing agent)}}}{O_2} \longrightarrow \underset{\text{Zinc oxide}}{2ZnO}$$

In the above reaction, oxygen reacts with zinc to form zinc oxide (oxygen gets added to zinc here). So, oxygen acts as an oxidizing agent here.

$$\underset{\substack{\text{Hydrogen} \\ \text{sulphide}}}{H_2S} + \underset{\substack{\text{Chlorine} \\ \text{(Oxidizing agent)}}}{Cl_2} \longrightarrow \underset{\text{Hydrogen chloride}}{2HCl} + \underset{\text{Sulphur}}{S}$$

In the above reaction, chlorine reacts with hydrogen sulphide to remove hydrogen from hydrogen sulphide and thus oxidizing sulphur. So, chlorine acts as an oxidizing agent here.

Reduction: The process of removal of oxygen or addition of hydrogen to a substance is known as **reduction** and the substance that removes oxygen or produces hydrogen is called a **reducing agent**.

$$\underset{\text{Copper oxide}}{CuO} + \underset{\substack{\text{Hydrogen} \\ \text{(Reducing agent)}}}{H_2} \longrightarrow \underset{\text{Copper}}{Cu} + \underset{\text{Water}}{H_2O}$$

In the above reaction, when hydrogen gas is passed over heated metal oxides, the oxides are reduced to the corresponding metals. So, hydrogen acts as a reducing agent here.

$$Cl_2 + H_2S \longrightarrow 2HCl + S$$

Chlorine + Hydrogen sulphide (Reducing agent) → Hydrogen chloride + Sulphur

In the above reaction, hydrogen sulphide reacts with chlorine to add hydrogen to chlorine. So, hydrogen sulphide acts as a reducing agent here.

The reactions in which both oxidation and reduction take place simultaneously are referred to as **redox reactions**.

1. In the reaction between lead oxide and hydrogen, hydrogen is oxidized to water and lead oxide is reduced to lead. This is a redox reaction as both reduction and oxidation take place simultaneously.

Oxidation (H_2 → H_2O)

$$PbO + H_2 \longrightarrow Pb + H_2O$$

Lead oxide + Hydrogen → Lead + Water

Reduction (PbO → Pb)

2. In the reaction between copper oxide and hydrogen, hydrogen is oxidized to water and copper oxide is reduced to copper. This is a redox reaction as both reduction and oxidation take place simultaneously.

Oxidation (H_2 → H_2O)

$$CuO + H_2 \longrightarrow Cu + H_2O$$

Copper oxide + Hydrogen → Copper + Water

Reduction (CuO → Cu)

Know the Scientist

Edward Teller (1908–2003), a Hungarian-born American theoretical physicist, is considered as 'the father of the hydrogen bomb' for his invention of the hydrogen bomb in the year 1951.

Revision Zone

Write T for True and F for False.

1. Hydrogen gas smells like rotten eggs.
2. Hydrogen reacts with oxygen to produce a pale blue-coloured flame.
3. Hydrogen gas changes blue litmus to red.
4. Hydrogen reacts with calcium to form calcium hydroxide.
5. In the reaction of copper oxide and hydrogen, copper oxide is reduced to copper.

Uses of Hydrogen

Common uses of hydrogen are as follows.

1. The liquid form of hydrogen is widely used as a rocket fuel.
2. It is used in cutting and welding of metals as **oxy-hydrogen flame**.
3. It is used in the preparation of ammonia through Haber's process. Ammonia produced by this method is used in the manufacture of explosives and fertilizers like urea.
4. It is used as a reducing agent in the extraction of pure metals from their oxides.
5. It is used in the **hydrogenation of oils** for the conversion of liquid vegetable oils into *vanaspati* and margarine in the presence of nickel as a catalyst.
6. It is used in the manufacture of petrol, methanol and hydrochloric acid.
7. It is used to fill balloons, which help to study weather conditions, such as, air pressure, temperature and wind speed.

▲ Oxy-hydrogen flame

▲ Urea

▲ Hydrogen-filled balloons

True Fact

Use of hydrogen fuel (a non-polluting fuel) instead of fossil fuels can help in reducing pollution and also in conserving fossil fuels.

Do You Know?

Due to the highly inflammable nature of hydrogen, helium gas (a non-inflammable gas) is preferred over hydrogen to fill balloons.

Know the Scientist

Jacques Alexander Cesar Charles (1746–1823), a French scientist, invented the hydrogen balloon in the year 1783. The world's first balloon filled with hydrogen was launched in August, 1783. He was the first person to fly in a hydrogen balloon along with Nicolas-Louis Robert. He also invented the valve to release hydrogen out of the balloon. Some of his other inventions are goniometer and hydrometer. The gas law called 'Charles' law' that explains the expansion of gases upon heating is named after him.

Revision Zone

Write T for True and F for False.

1. Hydrogen is used as an oxidizing agent in the extraction of pure metals from their oxides.
2. Liquid hydrogen is used as a rocket fuel.
3. Zinc is used as a catalyst in the conversion of vegetable oils into *vanaspati*.
4. Hydrogen is used in the manufacture of methanol.
5. Hydrogen balloons are used to study the weather.

Keywords

Electrolysis of water: the decomposition of water into oxygen and hydrogen due to the passage of electric current through water containing a small quantity of acid

Oxidation: the process of removal of hydrogen or addition of oxygen to a substance

Oxidizing agent: the substance that removes hydrogen or produces oxygen

Reduction: the process of removal of oxygen or addition of hydrogen to a substance

Reducing agent: the substance that removes oxygen or produces hydrogen

Redox reaction: a reaction in which both oxidation and reduction take place simultaneously

Hydrogenation of oils: the conversion of liquid vegetable oils into *vanaspati* using hydrogen in the presence of nickel as a catalyst

In a Nutshell

- Metals like sodium, potassium and calcium displace hydrogen from water and form respective hydroxides.
- Electrolysis of water is widely used in the industrial preparation of hydrogen.
- Metals react with dilute acids to displace hydrogen gas and form their respective salts.
- In the laboratory, hydrogen is prepared by the reaction of zinc granules with dilute hydrochloric acid or dilute sulphuric acid.
- Hydrogen is the lightest gas.
- Hydrogen is insoluble in water.
- Hydrogen reacts with highly reactive metals at high temperatures to form respective metal hydrides.
- Hydrogen being neutral does not change the colour of either blue litmus or red litmus.
- Hydrogen is used to produce ammonia through the Haber's process.
- Hydrogen reduces metal oxides to corresponding metals when it is passed over heated metal oxides, thus, acting as a reducing agent.

Exercise

1 Choose the correct answer for each of the following.

a. Complete the word equation given below:

Metal + dilute acids ⟶ Salt + __________

i. Water
ii. Hydrogen gas
iii. Carbon dioxide
iv. Carbon monoxide

b. Which statement describes a test for hydrogen gas?

i. It turns blue litmus paper red.
ii. It turns red litmus paper blue.
iii. It turns lime water cloudy.
iv. Lighted matchstick burns off with a 'pop' sound.

c. In the laboratory, hydrogen gas is prepared in large amounts by the reaction of __________.

i. zinc and dilute hydrochloric acid
ii. copper and dilute hydrochloric acid
iii. zinc and dilute nitric acid
iv. silver and dilute hydrochloric acid

d. Which of the following chemical reactions of hydrogen is also referred to as combustion?

i. Reaction of hydrogen with metals
ii. Reaction of hydrogen with sulphur
iii. Reaction of hydrogen with chlorine
iv. Reaction of hydrogen with oxygen

e. Hydrogen on reaction with sodium at high temperature forms

i. NaH ii. NaOH
iii. Na_2CO_3 iv. NaO

f. The reaction given below is known as __________.

$$3H_2 + N_2 \longrightarrow 2NH_3$$

i. hydrogenation
ii. Haber's process
iii. Bosch's process
iv. displacement reaction

2 Fill in the blanks.

a. The flame used in cutting and welding of metals is __________ (oxy-hydrogen flame/hydro-oxy flame).

b. The process of addition of hydrogen to a substance is __________ (oxidation/ reduction).

c. The reactions in which both oxidation and reduction take place simultaneously are referred to as __________ (redox reactions/displacement reactions).

d. Hydrogen reacts with metals at high temperatures to form respective __________ (metal hydroxides/ metal hydrides).

e. The catalyst used in the hydrogenation of oils is __________ (iron/nickel).

f. Hydrogen reacts with oxygen to produce a __________ (red-coloured/pale blue-coloured) flame.

g. The promoter used in the preparation of ammonia from hydrogen is __________ (magnesium/molybdenum).

3 Write T for True and F for False.

a. Hydrogen is a combustible gas but does not support the process of combustion.

b. Hydrogen exists abundantly on Earth in the combined form.

c. Nickel reacts with cold water to form nickel oxide and releases hydrogen gas.

d. Hydrogen acts as a reducing agent in all chemical reactions.

e. Hydrogen is neutral in nature.

f. Hydrogen is soluble in water.

g. Hydrogen is used in the manufacture of hydrochloric acid.

h. Hydrogen is a non-combustible gas.

4 Define the following terms.

a. Oxidizing agent

b. Electrolysis

c. Reducing agent

d. Redox reaction

e. Haber's process

5 Complete and balance the following equations.

a. $PbO + H_2 \longrightarrow$ ______

b. $Ca + \text{dil. } HCl \longrightarrow$ ______

c. $Zn + \text{dil. } H_2SO_4 \longrightarrow$ ______

d. $Na + H_2O \text{ (cold)} \longrightarrow$ ______

e. $Ca + H_2 \longrightarrow$ ______

6 Name the following.

a. The method used for the conversion of liquid vegetable oils into *vanaspati*.

b. The catalyst used in Haber's process.

c. Any two compounds in which hydrogen exists in combined form.

d. Any two metals that react vigorously with cold water and displace hydrogen.

e. The reactant reduced in the reaction between lead oxide and hydrogen.

7 Answer the following questions in brief.

a. Define displacement reaction with the help of an example.

b. How is hydrogen prepared from water using the method of electrolysis?

c. State the physical properties of hydrogen.

d. Explain the preparation of ammonia using hydrogen.

e. Distinguish between oxidation and reduction.

f. Explain the formation of metal hydrides from hydrogen.

8 Answer the following questions in detail.

a. 'Hydrogen acts as both oxidizing and reducing agents'. Justify the statement with an example.

b. Explain the occurrence of hydrogen.

c. Explain the preparation of hydrogen in the laboratory.

d. Explain any four chemical properties of hydrogen with equations.

e. Mention the various uses of hydrogen.

f. Explain how hydrogen is prepared by the displacement of dilute acids by metals.

g. Explain the preparation of hydrogen on reaction of sodium with water.

9 Think and answer.

Shalini has two different coloured balloons of the same size; one is filled with hydrogen and the other is filled with nitrogen. If she allows both the balloons to fly at the same time, which balloon will move up faster and why?

(Hint: Recall the physical properties of hydrogen.)

10 In the Library

a. Refer library books to find out about the procedure of hydrogenation of oils. Prepare a chart, discuss with your teacher and display the same on your school notice board.

b. Find out information about:

- Hydrogen fuel cells
- Disasters caused due to hydrogen gas explosions

Worksheet

Subject Integration

a. Madhav has two different coloured balloons of the same size. One of his balloons is filled with hydrogen gas and the other balloon with nitrogen gas. He released both the balloons at the same time. Which balloon will move up faster and why?

Balloon filled with hydrogen gas

Balloon filled with nitrogen gas

b. How are hydrogen-filled balloons used in the meteorological studies?

8

Water

What I shall learn

- Water cycle
- Properties of water
- Solutions, suspensions and colloids
- Unsaturated, saturated and supersaturated solutions
- Water of crystallization
- Hydrated, anhydrous and hygroscopic substances
- Reactivity of metals with cold water, hot water and steam
- Hard and soft water

Introduction

Water is one of the most essential components of life. It covers nearly 71 per cent of Earth's surface. Around 97 per cent of the water on Earth is present in seas and oceans, but it is not suitable for drinking and other uses as it has high salt content. The fresh water constitutes about 3 per cent of Earth's total water. The major part of the fresh water is frozen in glaciers and polar icecaps. Hence, only about 0.01 per cent of the total water on Earth is available for human consumption, irrigation and other uses.

Due to the increase in population and environmental pollution, there is a considerable decrease in the availability of freshwater on Earth. Pure drinking water has become a precious resource, which needs to be saved for future generations.

Water Cycle

The natural process in which there is a continuous circulation of water from Earth's surface to the atmosphere and back to Earth's surface is known as the **water cycle**. This happens repeatedly and in a particular order to form a cycle.

In this process, water gets converted into all the three states of matter (solid, liquid and gas) but in different stages. The various steps in the water cycle are shown in the figure on the next page.

Properties of Water

Water is a chemical compound made up of two elements: hydrogen and oxygen. These elements combine chemically in a fixed proportion (in the ratio of 2:1) to form a molecule of water. Therefore, the chemical formula of water is H_2O.

The properties of water molecule are different from those of its individual constituents (hydrogen and oxygen). The constituents of water cannot be separated by physical methods. However, on passing electric current, water decomposes into hydrogen and oxygen. This is called **electrolysis of water**.

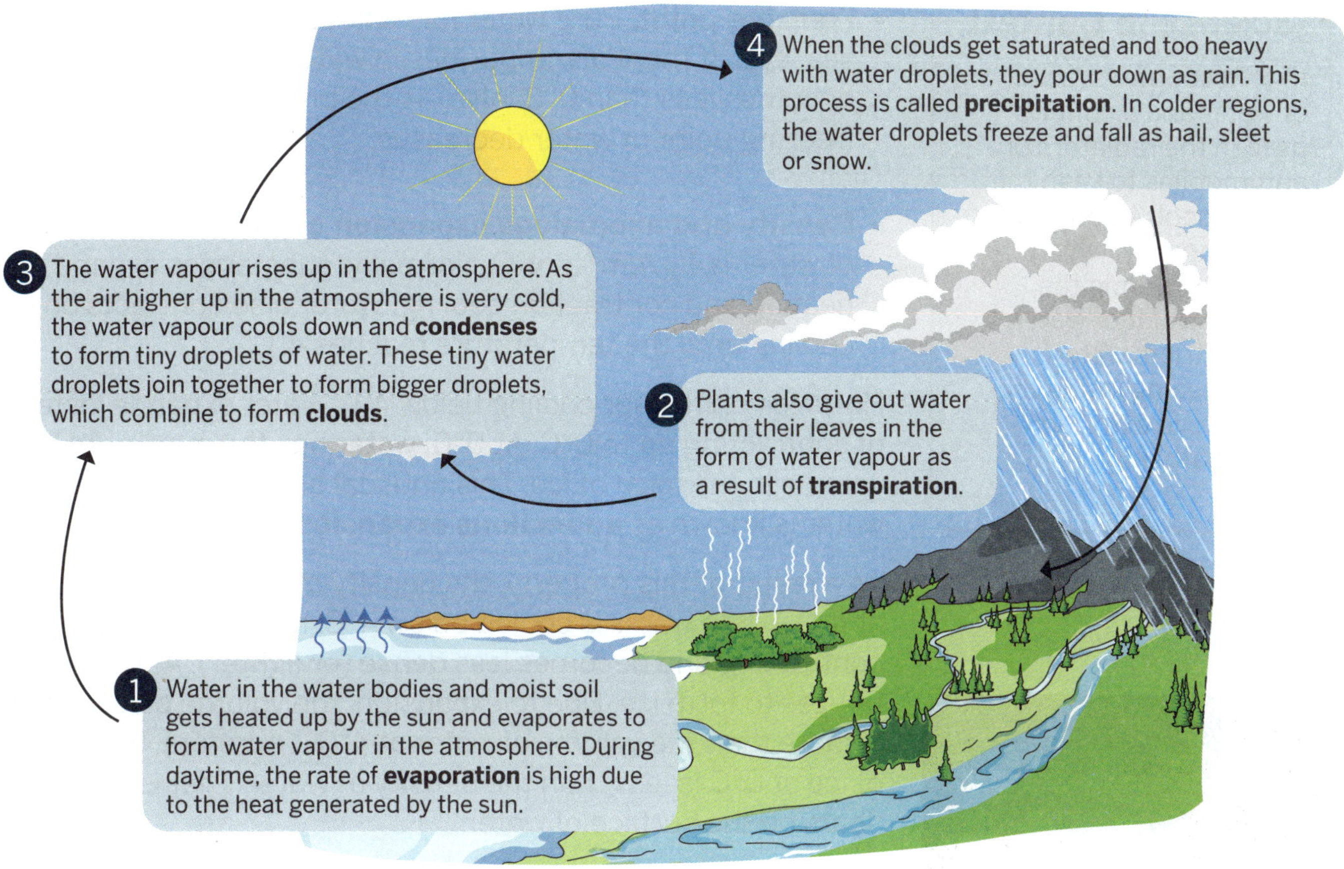

▲ Water cycle

Let us learn about some more properties of water.

- **Nature**: Water is colourless, tasteless, odourless and transparent in its pure form.
- **Forms of water**: We know that water exists in three different states in nature: solid, liquid and gas. The three states of water are interchangeable, that is, water can be changed from one form to another by changing the temperature.

Challenge Yourself

Why does it take longer to cook food in the hills than in the plains?

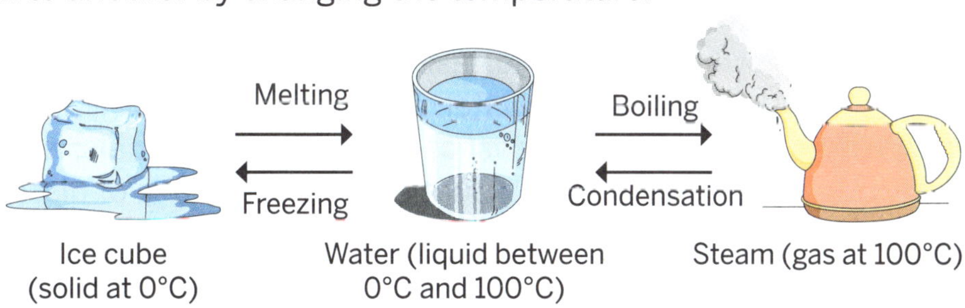

▲ Forms of water

- **Conductivity**: Pure water does not conduct heat and electricity. Water only conducts electricity if there are dissolved impurities (salts and minerals) present in it.
- **Boiling point**: Pure water has a boiling point of 100°C at sea level. Atmospheric pressure and the presence of dissolved impurities have an impact on the boiling point of water. At high pressure, the boiling point of water increases, to more than 100°C, while it decreases at low pressure. If there are impurities present in water, it boils at a higher temperature.

- **Freezing point**: Pure water has a freezing point of 0°C at sea level. If there are impurities in water, the freezing point becomes less than 0°C. Also, as the pressure increases, the freezing point of water decreases.

- **Density and anomalous expansion of water**: The density of water is 1 g/cm^3 at 4°C. Normally, substances expand on heating and contract on cooling. Water also contracts on cooling until the temperature reaches 4°C.

However, on further cooling below 4°C, water expands instead of contracting up to 0°C. At 0°C, water has the maximum volume in the form of ice. This unusual and unique property of water is known as **anomalous expansion** of water.

As a result of this property, the density of water is maximum at 4°C. When water is cooled below 4°C, it expands instead of contracting and becomes less dense (or lighter). At 0°C, water freezes to form ice. Due to expansion, the volume of ice at 0°C is more than the volume of water at 4°C. Therefore, the density of ice at 0°C is less than the density of water. That is why, ice floats on the surface of water.

Effects of anomalous expansion of water: In cold regions, where atmospheric temperature falls to 0°C or below, water on the surface of ponds and lakes cools and freezes into ice. The frozen ice floats on the surface of the water as the density of ice is less than the density of water. As water is a bad conductor of heat, the ice layer prevents loss of heat from the lower layers of water. Thus, water below the layer of floating ice has temperatures greater than 0°C, which helps in the survival of aquatic life present underneath.

- **Gases dissolved in water and their importance:** Atmospheric gases like oxygen and carbon dioxide can dissolve in water. Dissolved oxygen, which is very important for the survival of many aquatic animals, is used for respiration. Aquatic plants make use of dissolved carbon dioxide to prepare food and release oxygen which is used by fishes.

Soft drinks contain carbon dioxide gas dissolved in water at high pressure in which carbon dioxide is the solute and water is the solvent. Apart from oxygen and carbon dioxide, other gases like ammonia, chlorine, methane and nitrogen can also dissolve in water.

- **Water contains dissolved solids**: Substances like salts, minerals, metals or ions, which are called the TDS (Total Dissolved Solids), dissolve in water.

Science in Context

In cold countries, a mixture of water and alcohol is used in the radiators of automobiles to keep the engine cool. Alcohol acts as an impurity, which helps in lowering the freezing point of water. This restricts water from freezing inside the radiators in extremely cold weather.

$$\text{Density} = \frac{\text{Mass}}{\text{Volume}}$$

▲ Floating of ice on water

Science in Context

The cracks observed in the water supply pipes in cold regions are due to the anomalous expansion of water when it freezes at 0°C. On freezing, water expands and occupies more space than liquid water. This results in cracking of water pipes.

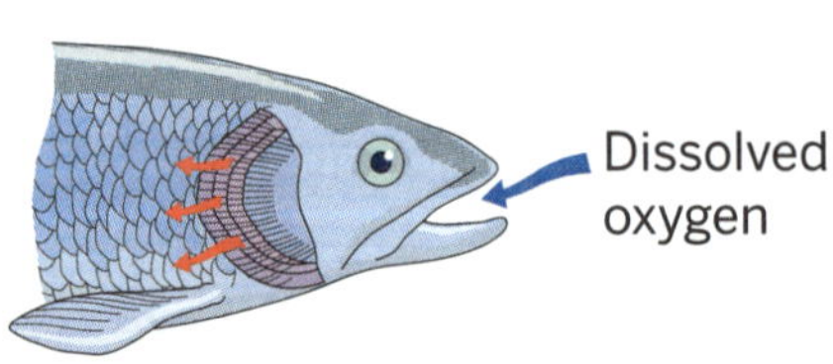

▲ Aquatic animals use dissolved oxygen

- The nutrients present in the soil and the food prepared by the leaves of plants are transported to other parts of the plants in the form of solution.
- Water acts as a medium to dissolve nutrients and minerals present in the food that living things eat. This helps in the easy absorption of nutrients by the body. The absorbed food and nutrients are carried to various parts of the body through the blood.
- Even the waste products in our body like sweat and urine are soluble in water and are excreted out from the body in the form of water.

Water—A Universal Solvent

Water can dissolve a greater variety of substances than any other liquid. Hence, water is also called the **universal solvent**. All substances do not dissolve in water. For example, when salt is added to water and stirred, it dissolves completely in water, but sand does not dissolve in water.

Substances that dissolve completely in water are said to be **soluble** in water. Substances that do not dissolve in water are said to be **insoluble** in water.

Similarly, liquids that dissolve in water are called **miscible** liquids, e.g., vinegar and alcohol. Liquids that do not dissolve in water are called **immiscible** liquids, e.g., oil and petrol.

Activity 1

Aim: To test the dissolving capacity of water with various salts

Materials required: Four glass beakers, measuring cylinder, weighing balance, four glass rods, spatula, sodium chloride, potassium chloride, sodium carbonate, calcium carbonate and water

Procedure:

1. Take 20 ml of water in each of the four glass beakers.
2. Label the beakers as 1, 2, 3 and 4.
3. In beaker 1, add 2 g of sodium chloride (which was weighed and kept using a weighing balance).
4. In beaker 2, add 2 g of potassium chloride.
5. In beaker 3, add 2 g of sodium carbonate.
6. In beaker 4, add 2 g of calcium carbonate.
7. Mix the contents of the glass beakers with the help of a glass rod. Use separate glass rods for each beaker and observe.

Observation:

- Sodium chloride; potassium chloride and sodium carbonate salts dissolve in water, whereas calcium carbonate does not dissolve in water but gets settled at the bottom of the beaker.
- Potassium chloride dissolves in water completely faster than sodium chloride, followed by sodium carbonate.

Conclusion: From this activity, we can conclude that different salts have different solubility in water.

Revision Zone

Write T for True and F for False.

1. The three states of water are interchangeable.
2. Water contracts on cooling until the temperature reaches 40°C.
3. All substances dissolve in water.
4. Aquatic animals survive with the help of dissolved oxygen.
5. Impurities do not affect the freezing point of water.

Solutions

Let us recall the following terms related to solutions.

- The substance that dissolves (smaller component) is called the **solute**.
- The substance in which the solute dissolves (larger component) is called the **solvent**.
- The solute dissolves in the solvent to form a **solution**. Thus, a solution is a uniform mixture of a solute in a solvent. Solutions are homogeneous mixtures.
- The property of a substance to dissolve in a given liquid is known as the **solubility** of that substance.

Examples of solutions:

1. Soda: Carbon dioxide is the solute, water is the solvent.
2. Tincture: Iodine is the solute, alcohol is the solvent.
3. Glucose solution: Glucose is the solute, water is the solvent.
4. Copper sulphate solution: Copper sulphate is the solute, water is the solvent.
5. Salt solution: Salt is the solute, water is the solvent.

Unsaturated, Saturated and Supersaturated Solutions

Difference between unsaturated, saturated and supersaturated solutions is given in the following table.

Table 8.1 Difference between unsaturated, saturated and supersaturated solutions

Unsaturated solution	Saturated solution	Supersaturated solution
A solution in which solute concentration is low and more solute can be dissolved in the solvent at a given temperature is called an **unsaturated solution**. An unsaturated solution contains less amount of dissolved solute than a saturated solution.	A solution in which no more solute can be dissolved in the solvent at a given temperature is called a **saturated solution**. A saturated solution contains the maximum amount of dissolved solute at the given temperature.	A solution in which there is more amount of solute in the solvent at a given temperature is called a **supersaturated solution**. A supersaturated solution contains more amount of dissolved solute than a saturated solution.

Suspensions

Suspensions are heterogeneous mixtures. The particles in a suspension are larger than that of a solution and these particles can be separated by filtration process. A suspension contains small, undissolved solid particles suspended in a fluid (a liquid or a gas). These particles can be seen distinctly. When the suspension is kept undisturbed, the particles settle down.

Examples of suspensions:

- Sand in water
- Powdered chalk in water
- Dust in air
- Soot in air
- Oil in water

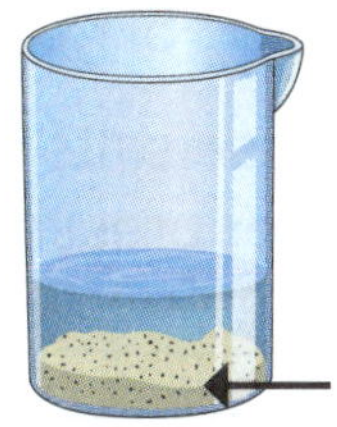

▲ Sand particles settle at the bottom of the beaker

Colloids

Colloids are heterogeneous mixtures. Every colloid contains two parts — colloidal particles (dispersed phase) and dispersing medium. The particles of colloids (solid or liquid) will have intermediate size between suspension and solution particles.

The particles of colloids do not dissolve but get dispersed in the medium and cannot be separated by filtration. The particles can scatter light due to the large size of the particles. For instance, we are able to observe the light from car headlamps through fog.

Examples of colloids:

- Milk (dispersed phase: liquid; dispersed medium: liquid)
- Fog (dispersed phase: solid; dispersed medium: gas)
- Insecticide sprays (dispersed phase: solid; dispersed medium: gas)
- Soap lather (dispersed phase: gas; dispersed medium: liquid)

Milk

Fog

▲ Examples of colloids

Table 8.2 Differences between suspensions and colloids

Suspensions	Colloids
• Suspensions are heterogeneous mixtures.	• Colloids are heterogeneous mixtures but sometimes exhibit the properties of homogeneous mixtures.
• The size of the particles is large, thus visible to the naked eye.	• The size of the particles is very small and microscopic.
• The particles get settled on keeping undisturbed.	• The particles do not settle on standing.
• Suspensions can be separated by filtration.	• Colloids cannot be separated by filtration.
• Examples: Sand in water, oil in water	• Examples: Milk and fog

Water of Crystallization

Some of the salts contain water molecules trapped inside them. The fixed number of water molecules available in one formula unit of a salt is known as **water of crystallization**.

Examples: $CuSO_4 \cdot 5H_2O$, $CaSO_4 \cdot 2H_2O$, $Na_2CO_3 \cdot 10H_2O$, $Na_2SO_4 \cdot 10H_2O$, $FeSO_4 \cdot 7H_2O$

The water in these salts is responsible for the shape of the crystals. When these crystals are heated, the water present in the salts is lost.

Activity 2

Aim: To observe the loss of water of crystallization in hydrated copper sulphate

Materials required: Copper sulphate crystals, Bunsen burner, spatula

Procedure:

1. Take hydrated copper sulphate crystals in a clean spatula.
2. Start heating the copper sulphate crystals over Bunsen burner.

Observation: The blue colour of the copper sulphate crystals change into white after heating.

Conclusion: The change in colour is observed due to the dehydration process (the removal of water molecules trapped in the copper sulphate crystals due to heating).

Hydrated, Anhydrous and Hygroscopic Substances

Hydrated Substances: Substances that contain water of crystallization in them are referred to as **hydrated substances**.

Examples:

- Magnesium sulphate ($MgSO_4 \cdot 7H_2O$): Epsom salt
- Ferrous sulphate ($FeSO_4 \cdot 7H_2O$): Green vitriol
- Copper (II) sulphate ($CuSO_4 \cdot 5H_2O$): Blue vitriol
- Calcium sulphate ($CaSO_4 \cdot 2H_2O$): Gypsum

Anhydrous Substances: Substances that do not contain water of crystallization in them are referred to as **anhydrous substances**.

For instance, when we heat copper sulphate crystals ($CuSO_4 \cdot 5H_2O$), the water molecules will get evaporated .The remaining salt without water is referred to as anhydrous salt. Now the anhydrous salt's formula will be $CuSO_4$.

$$\underset{\text{Hydrated copper sulphate}}{CuSO_4 \cdot 5H_2O} \xrightarrow{\text{Heating}} \underset{\text{Anhydrous copper sulphate}}{CuSO_4} + 5H_2O$$

Hygroscopic Substances: Substances that are capable of attracting water from their surroundings are referred to as **hygroscopic substances**.

Examples: Zinc chloride, calcium chloride, potassium hydroxide, sodium chloride and sodium hydroxide crystals are a few examples of hygroscopic substances.

Revision Zone

Fill in the blanks with the correct words.

1. Solutions are an example of ________ (homogeneous/heterogeneous) mixtures.
2. Suspensions are an example of ________ (homogeneous/heterogeneous) mixtures.
3. In glucose solution, ________ (glucose/water) is the solute and ________ (glucose/water) is the solvent.
4. Milk is an example of ________ (suspension/colloid).
5. Sand in water is an example of ________ (suspension/colloid).
6. Substances that are capable of attracting water from their surroundings are known as ________ (hygroscopic/anhydrous)substances.

Reaction of Metals with Water

Metals react with water to form metal oxides or metal hydroxides and hydrogen gas.

$$\text{Metal} + \text{Water} \longrightarrow \text{Metal oxide or Metal hydroxide} + \text{Hydrogen gas}$$

Metals like potassium, sodium and calcium react vigorously with cold water to form their respective hydroxides and release hydrogen gas. A large amount of heat is also released. Reactions in which heat is released are called **exothermic reactions**.

- Sodium reacts with cold water to form sodium hydroxide and hydrogen gas.

$$\underset{\text{Sodium}}{2Na} + \underset{\text{Water}}{2H_2O} \longrightarrow \underset{\text{Sodium hydroxide}}{2NaOH} + \underset{\text{Hydrogen}}{H_2(g)}$$

▲ Reaction of sodium with water

The release of a large amount of heat in the above reaction makes the hydrogen gas to catch fire as shown in the figure given alongside. Thus, sodium is stored in kerosene because of its vigorous reaction with water.

- Zinc reacts only with steam to form zinc oxide and releases hydrogen gas.

$$\underset{\text{Zinc}}{Zn} + \underset{\text{Steam}}{H_2O(g)} \longrightarrow \underset{\text{Zinc oxide}}{ZnO} + \underset{\text{Hydrogen}}{H_2(g)}$$

Science in Context

Aluminium does not react with water because as soon as it is exposed to air, it reacts and forms a layer of oxide (aluminium oxide) on its surface and prevents further reaction from taking place.

- Magnesium reacts with steam to form magnesium oxide and releases hydrogen gas.

$$\underset{\text{Magnesium}}{Mg} + \underset{\text{Steam}}{H_2O\,(g)} \longrightarrow \underset{\text{Magnesium oxide}}{MgO} + \underset{\text{Hydrogen}}{H_2\,(g)}$$

- Metals that are placed lower in the reactivity series like platinum, gold, silver and copper do not react with water at all.

Do You Know?

Gold and platinum are widely used in jewellery because they do not react with oxygen and water. They do not tarnish or undergo oxidation. Hence, they are extremely durable.

Know the Fact

Phosphorus, a very reactive non-metal that can catch fire when exposed to air, is actually stored in water as it does not react with water.

Magnesium oxide is slightly soluble in water. Magnesium hydroxide (Milk of magnesia) is the product formed during the reaction between magnesium oxide and water.

$$MgO + H_2O \longrightarrow Mg(OH)_2$$

The above reaction can be reversed by heating the mixture to remove the moisture.

The reaction between calcium hydroxide and water is highly vigorous and exothermic to form calcium oxide (slaked lime).

$$CaO + H_2O \longrightarrow Ca(OH)_2$$

Note: Generally non-metals do not react with water under any conditions.

Activity 3

Note: This activity needs to be performed as a teacher demonstration.

Aim: To conclude that metals react with water whereas non-metals do not

Materials required: Two 250 mℓ glass beakers, cold water, small pieces of sodium and charcoal, knife, forceps

Procedure:

1. Take a clean 250 mℓ glass beaker and fill it with 100 mℓ of cold water.
2. Cut a small piece of sodium using a knife and dry it with a filter paper.
3. With the help of a tong or forceps, slowly drop the piece of sodium metal into the beaker containing cold water.
4. Try to touch the beaker after the reaction is over. Ensure that the reaction is no longer taking place and touch it from a safe distance.
5. Repeat the above activity with a charcoal piece in a separate beaker and record your observations.

Observation table:

S.No.	Sample	Observation
	Sodium piece	Release of heat, gas and light would be observed. When touched, we can feel the surface of the beaker to be hot.
	Charcoal piece	No reaction would be observed.

Conclusion: Sodium, being a metal, reacts with water, and charcoal, being a non-metal, does not react with water.

Hard Water and Soft Water

Soft water is the water that easily gives lather with the use of soap and is free from salts of magnesium and calcium.

Hard water is the water that contains high amount of dissolved salts and does not give lather with the use of soap. It results in the formation of a thick, dirty layer (curd-like, insoluble substance) on the surface of water known as **scum**.

How Hardness is Caused

Hardness of water is caused due to the presence of salts of magnesium and calcium dissolved in it.

Hardness of water is of two types.

- **Temporary hardness**: Temporary hardness of water is due to the presence of dissolved bicarbonates of magnesium and calcium in it.
- **Permanent hardness**: Permanent hardness of water is due to the presence of dissolved sulphates and chlorides of magnesium and calcium in it.

Activity 4

Aim: To analyze water samples for their hardness

Materials required: Distilled water, hard water, soap solution and glass test tubes

Note: Hard water can be prepared by adding a pinch of magnesium chloride in distilled water.

Procedure:

1. Take two glass test tubes and label them as 1 and 2.
2. Take 10 $m\ell$ of distilled water in test tube 1 and 10 $m\ell$ of hard water in test tube 2.
3. Add 5-6 drops of soap solution into each of the test tubes and gently mix the contents of the test tubes.
4. Observe the contents of the test tubes and record your observations.

Conclusion: Test tube 1 that contains distilled water gives lather. Whereas, test tube 2 containing hard water does not show any lather formation and a layer of curd-like scum can be seen on its surface.

Drawbacks of Hard Water

- Hard water is unfit for drinking and cooking purposes.
- It is also not suitable for washing clothes as it results in the wastage of soap. Further, the scum formed leaves stains on clothes.
- In industries that use hard water, the deposits of magnesium and calcium salts formed at high temperatures result in scale formation in the machine parts. This may also lead to the explosion of boilers and minimize the heating efficiency of radiators.
- Scale formation may result in the blockage of water pipes that are used for the transportation of hard water.

Methods of Softening Hard Water

The process of removing dissolved salts of magnesium and calcium from hard water to get soft water is called the **softening of water**.

It can be done by the following methods.

- **By boiling**: Temporary hardness of water can be easily removed by boiling.

  On boiling, the magnesium and calcium bicarbonates are converted into their respective carbonates. These carbonates are insoluble in nature and can be removed by filtration to obtain soft water.

$Mg(HCO_3)_2$	$\xrightarrow{\text{Heat}}$	$MgCO_3$	+	H_2O	+	CO_2
Magnesium bicarbonate		Magnesium carbonate		Water		Carbon dioxide

$Ca(HCO_3)_2$	$\xrightarrow{\text{Heat}}$	$CaCO_3$	+	H_2O	+	CO_2
Calcium bicarbonate		Calcium carbonate		Water		Carbon dioxide

  Permanent hardness of water cannot be removed by boiling because the salts (chlorides and sulphates of calcium and magnesium) are stable to heat.

- **By treating with chemicals like washing soda (Na_2CO_3)**: Permanent hardness of water can be removed by adding washing soda or sodium carbonate.

  During this process, the sulphates and chlorides of magnesium and calcium are converted into their respective carbonates. These carbonates are insoluble in nature and can be removed by the filtration process to obtain soft water.

$MgSO_4$	+	Na_2CO_3	$\longrightarrow$	$MgCO_3$	+	Na_2SO_4
Magnesium sulphate		Sodium carbonate		Magnesium carbonate		Sodium sulphate
$CaCl_2$	+	Na_2CO_3	$\longrightarrow$	$CaCO_3$	+	$2NaCl$
Calcium chloride		Sodium carbonate		Calcium carbonate		Sodium chloride

The addition of washing soda to the bicarbonate of calcium can also remove temporary hardness of water to obtain soft water.

$$Ca(HCO_3)_2 + Na_2CO_3 \longrightarrow CaCO_3 + 2NaHCO_3$$

Calcium bicarbonate	Sodium carbonate	Calcium carbonate	Sodium bicarbonate

Keywords

Solution: a solution is a uniform mixture of a solute in a solvent

Solubility: the property of a substance to dissolve in a given liquid

Hydrated substances: the substances that contain water molecules within them

Anhydrous substances: the substances that do not contain water molecules within them

Hygroscopic substances: the substances that are capable of attracting water from their surroundings

Water of crystallization: the fixed number of water molecules available in one formula unit of a salt

Soft water: water that easily gives lather with the use of soap and is free from salts of magnesium and calcium

Hard water: water that does not give lather with the use of soap

In a Nutshell

- Water is an essential constituent of all living things for their survival.
- The continuous movement of water from Earth's surface to the atmosphere and back to Earth's surface is known as the water cycle.
- Water has many properties. One unique property of water is called the anomalous expansion of water. On cooling below 4°C, water expands instead of contracting up to 0°C. At 0°C, water has the maximum volume in the form of ice.
- The presence of impurities affects the boiling point and the freezing point of water.
- Water can dissolve a greater variety of different substances than any other liquid. Hence, water is also called the universal solvent.
- Hard water is the water that does not give lather with the use of soap. It results in the formation of a thick, dirty layer on the surface of the water known as scum.
- The softening of hard water can be done by the process of boiling and by the addition of washing soda.

Exercise

1. **Choose the correct answer for each of the following.**

   a. Which of these is not a property of water?
      i. Colourless
      ii. Conductivity
      iii. Opaque
      iv. Universal solvent

   b. Which of the following metals reacts vigorously with water?
      i. Gold ii. Silver
      iii. Potassium iv. Platinum

   c. Which of these is used to soften water?
      i. Bleaching powder
      ii. Calcium carbonate
      iii. Sodium chloride
      iv. Washing soda

   d. Which of the following is an example of a suspension?
      i. Milk ii. Soda
      iii. Oil in water iv. Fog

   e. Which of the following causes temporary hardness in water?
      i. Bicarbonates of magnesium
      ii. Chlorides of calcium
      iii. Sulphates of magnesium
      iv. Nitrates of potassium

2. **Fill in the blanks.**

   a. The process of separating insoluble impurities present in water is known as __________ (sedimentation/ chlorination).

   b. Water that does not give lather with soap is __________ (hard water/ soft water).

   c. Water fit for drinking is called __________ (potable/portable) water.

   d. Colloid is a __________ (homogeneous/heterogeneous) mixture.

   e. Substances that contain water molecules within them are referred to as __________ (hydrated/anhydrous) substances.

   f. The substance present in larger component in the solution is known as __________. (solute/solvent)

   g. __________ (Water filter/Boiling) is the easiest method to remove temporary hardness of water.

3. **Write T for True and F for False.**

   a. Pure water is a good conductor of electricity.

   b. The density of ice at 0°C is less than the density of water.

   c. Large amount of heat is released when potassium reacts with water.

   d. Magnesium reacts with cold water to form magnesium oxide and hydrogen gas.

   e. Nickel reacts with cold water to form nickel oxide and releases hydrogen gas.

   f. Sulphates and chlorides of magnesium and calcium cause temporary hardness of water.

4. **Define the following terms.**

   a. Universal solvent
   b. Water cycle
   c. Anomalous expansion of water
   d. Suspensions
   e. Colloids

5. **Differentiate between the following.**

   a. Miscible liquids and immiscible liquids
   b. Soft water and hard water

c. Temporary hardness and permanent hardness
d. Boiling point of water and freezing point of water
e. Unsaturated and saturated solution

6 Choose the odd one out. Give reasons for the choice.

a. Magnesium sulphate, calcium sulphate, magnesium chloride, magnesium bicarbonate
b. Glaciers, dew, snow, hail
c. Vinegar, alcohol, acetic acid, oil
d. Sand in water, powdered chalk in water, Fog, Dust in air
e. Soap lather, Insecticide sprays, Milk, Oil in water

7 Answer the following questions in brief.

a. Why is water called the universal solvent? Explain with an example.
b. Write any two drawbacks of hard water.
c. Distinguish between suspensions and colloids.
d. Differentiate between hydrated, anhydrous and hygroscopic substances.

8 Answer the following questions in detail.

a. Explain how water is circulated in the nature.
b. List the properties of water and briefly explain each.
c. Explain the importance of the property of anomalous expansion of water.
d. What are the methods used for softening hard water?
e. Explain about water of crystallization.
f. Explain the reaction of metals with cold water, hot water and steam with an example for each.

9 Think and answer.

You are given two unlabelled containers. One of them contains pure water and the other contains impure water, but the water in both the containers looks the same. How will you identify the container that contains impure water?

Note: You are not supposed to taste or touch the contents of any of the containers. (Hint: Recall the properties of water.)

10 Project

Try to visit a nearby water treatment plant and collect information about the various processes that are followed in the purification of water. Prepare a report on your observations and submit it to your teacher.

11 In the Library

Collect information from the library about the Ganga Action Plan. Prepare a comprehensive report on the aim, plan of action, results and the conclusion to be drawn from them.

Worksheet

Answer the following.

a. Identify the following as solutions, suspensions and colloids.

Name	**Type**
Milk	
Salt and water	
Mayonnaise and water	
Muddy water	
Coconut oil and water	
Soda	
Powdered chalk and water	
Tincture	
Sand and water	

b. Write any two differences between suspensions and colloids.

____

____

____

____

c. Depict the quantity of solute in the following.

Saturated solution	Supersaturated solution	Unsaturated solution

Carbon and Its Compounds

9

What I shall learn

- Occurrence of carbon
- Crystalline forms of carbon
- Amorphous forms of carbon
- Carbon dioxide: Preparation, properties and uses
- Carbon monoxide: Properties, uses and harmful effects

Introduction

Carbon is the fourth most abundant element in the universe and the fifteenth most abundant element in the Earth's crust. The name carbon comes from the Latin word *carbo* meaning 'coal'. It is present in all living things like human beings, plants, animals and even in non-living things like wood, petroleum, coal, natural gas and plastics. Due to its chemical nature, carbon forms various compounds with other elements. It is a non-metal and is represented by the symbol 'C'.

Majority of the things that we use in our everyday lives contain carbon, for example, food, clothes, fuels, medicines, paper, plastics, etc.

In this chapter, we will learn about the occurrence, properties, various forms and uses of carbon.

Science in Context

Carbon forms the largest number of compounds. A separate branch of chemistry that deals with the study of carbon compounds is referred to as organic chemistry.

Occurrence of Carbon

Carbon exists both in the free state and in the combined state in nature. In the free state, carbon is mainly found in three forms: diamond, graphite and coal. In the combined state, carbon exists in the form of numerous organic and inorganic compounds. Table 9.1 lists a few organic and inorganic compounds of carbon.

Table 9.1 Few organic and inorganic compounds of carbon

Organic compounds of carbon	
Food nutrients	Carbohydrates, proteins, fats and vitamins are the important nutrients of food, which are present in both plants and animals. All these are organic compounds that mainly consist of carbon, hydrogen and oxygen atoms.
Carbohydrates	Glucose, cellulose, starch and other sugars are the various forms of carbohydrates. All these are made up of carbon, hydrogen and oxygen atoms. Cellulose is the most abundant organic compound on Earth.
Hydrocarbons	These are organic compounds that contain only carbon and hydrogen atoms, for example, methane (CH_4) and ethane (C_2H_6). Petroleum and natural gas are the

	important hydrocarbons found in nature as fossil fuels and are widely used as fuels. The main constituent of natural gas is methane.
Acids and alcohols	Carbon is an essential constituent of many acids and alcohols. For example, carbonic acid (H_2CO_3), acetic acid (CH_3COOH), methyl alcohol (CH_3OH), ethyl alcohol (C_2H_5OH), etc.
Inorganic compounds of carbon	
Carbon dioxide	It exists abundantly in the atmosphere (about 0.03% by volume) and is the major gaseous compound of carbon present in the air. It is soluble in water and is present as dissolved carbon dioxide in water bodies.
Carbon monoxide	It is another gaseous compound of carbon present in the air. It is formed during combustion of fuels in vehicles and factories.
Salts	Mineral salts like carbonates and bicarbonates are important carbon compounds found in nature. For example, $CaCO_3$ (chalk, limestone, marble), $MgCO_3$ (magnesite), Na_2CO_3 (washing soda), $NaHCO_3$ (baking soda) and $Ca(HCO_3)_2$.

Allotropy

Do You Know?

Carbon is widely used to find out the age of archaeological specimens through carbon-dating.

The property of an element to exist in various physical forms in the same physical state with identical chemical properties but different physical properties is known as **allotropy**. Carbon, oxygen, sulphur and phosphorus are a few elements that exhibit allotropy. The different physical forms in which an element can exist are called **allotropes** or **allotropic forms** of that element.

Carbon exists in two allotropic forms, which are the crystalline form and the amorphous form. Table 9.2 lists some differences between the crystalline and the amorphous forms of carbon.

Table 9.2 Differences between crystalline and amorphous forms of carbon

Crystalline form	Amorphous form
This form has a regular shape and size.	This form does not have a regular shape and size.
In this form, the carbon atoms are arranged in a definite repeating order or geometrical pattern. It also has sharp edges and plane surfaces and is thus known as a crystal.	In this form, the carbon atoms are not arranged in a definite order or geometrical pattern. It does not have sharp edges and plane surfaces. It is also known as the non-crystalline form of carbon.
It has fixed melting and boiling points.	It does not have any fixed melting and boiling points.
Examples: diamond, graphite and fullerenes.	Examples: charcoal, lampblack, coke and coal.

Science in Context

Crystals are solid substances that have definite geometrical forms and sharp edges in which constituent ions, atoms or molecules are arranged in a regular repeating pattern that extends in all directions. The study of crystals and their formation is known as **crystallography**.

Crystalline Forms of Carbon

Diamond, graphite and fullerene are the crystalline forms of carbon.

Diamond

Diamond is the purest form of carbon and is the hardest known naturally occurring substance. Due to extreme hardness, diamond is used in cutting tools. As a result, only a diamond can cut another diamond.

▲ Diamond

Occurrence of Diamond

Diamond mines are found in various parts of the world such as South Africa, Brazil, Angola, Ghana and India. South Africa is the leading producer and supplier of about 70 per cent of the world's diamonds. In India, diamonds are widely found in the Kollur mines in Andhra Pradesh and the Panna mines in Madhya Pradesh.

Naturally, diamonds are produced from carbon that has been subjected to very high pressure and temperature about 150 km below the Earth's surface. Through natural processes, these diamonds come to the surface of Earth, which are then mined. Diamonds are measured in **carats**, which is one-fifth of a gram.

Do You Know?

Kohinoor, the famous diamond, was mined from the Kollur mines in the Guntur district of Andhra Pradesh.

Synthetic diamonds: They are prepared through artificial processes in which pure carbon is compressed under extremely high pressure and temperature conditions; hence, they are also known as artificial or cultivated diamonds. They are widely used in polishing, grinding and cutting tools.

Structure of Diamond

In a diamond, each carbon atom is connected to four other carbon atoms by strong chemical bonds. This forms a tetrahedral shape in which one carbon atom lies at the centre and the four surrounding carbon atoms lie at the four corners of the tetrahedron.

Tetrahedral structure

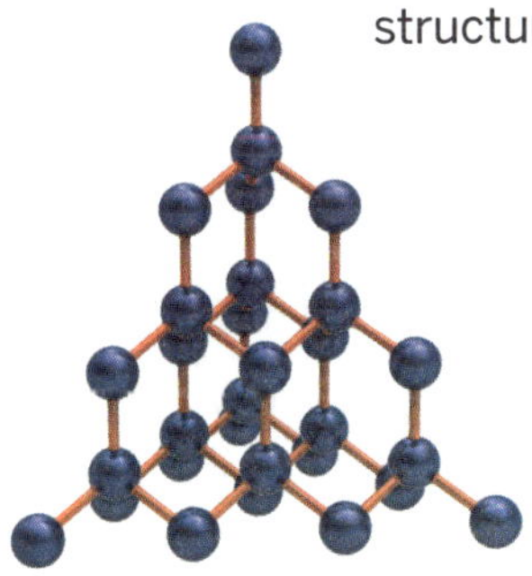

▲ Structure of diamond

Each of the four carbon atoms at the corners is further attached to four other carbon atoms, thus extending the tetrahedral arrangement. Each carbon atom is at an equal distance from its neighbouring carbon atoms and is thus held firmly in its place.

Due to the closely-packed and rigid arrangement of these carbon atoms, a diamond crystal is a rigid, three-dimensional structure. That is why, a diamond is hard in nature and has a high density and a high melting point.

Properties of Diamond

Do You Know?

Due to the presence of some metallic impurities in them, diamonds occur in various colours such as blue, green, yellow, red, grey, etc.

- Diamond is the hardest known naturally occurring substance on Earth.
- Pure diamonds are colourless, lustrous and crystalline solids. They are transparent in appearance.
- It has a high refractive index, which gives a diamond its sparkling appearance.
- It has a high density (3.5 g/cm^3) and a high melting point (about 3550°C).
- It is a poor conductor of electricity.
- When heated to about 800°C in the presence of oxygen, diamonds form carbon dioxide.
- It is insoluble in all solvents and is chemically inactive.
- The beauty and shine of a diamond depends on the way it is cut and polished.

Uses of Diamond

- Diamonds are widely used as precious gems in jewellery. Their powder is used to polish other diamonds and precious stones.
- They are used in drilling of hard rocks and cutting of glass.
- They are used as surgical tools by eye surgeons for removing cataract from eyes.
- Black or grey diamonds (called carbonado and bort) are used in the manufacture of high precision thermometers.
- They are used in the manufacture of radiation-proof windows in space satellites and spacecraft.

Graphite

Graphite, another crystalline form of carbon, is a dark grey or black, opaque solid. It is lighter than diamond and soft and slippery to touch. The word graphite is derived from the Greek word *gréphein*, which means 'to write or draw'.

Occurrence of Graphite

Graphite is abundantly found in various parts of the world such as Sri Lanka, Russia, China, India, North Korea, New York, Canada and Mexico. In India, large amounts of graphite are mined in Andhra Pradesh, Jammu and Kashmir, Uttar Pradesh, Rajasthan, Jharkhand, Kerala and Tamil Nadu.

Graphite is prepared synthetically by heating coke at a temperature of 3000°C.

Structure of Graphite

In graphite, carbon atoms are arranged in the form of flat plane layers or sheets. In each layer, every carbon atom is attached to three other carbon atoms by strong chemical bonds which form flat hexagonal rings. Each hexagonal ring is made up of six carbon atoms.

The different layers of carbon atoms in graphite are linked to each other by weak forces of attraction. As a result, these layers can slip over each other, giving graphite its soft and slippery texture.

A carbon atom has four valence electrons (atomic number = 6, valency = 4). This means it can form four bonds. In the crystal structure of graphite, each carbon atom is linked to only three other carbon atoms. This implies that the fourth valence electron of each carbon atom remains free to move around inside its crystal structure. The presence of these free electrons in graphite makes it a good conductor of electricity.

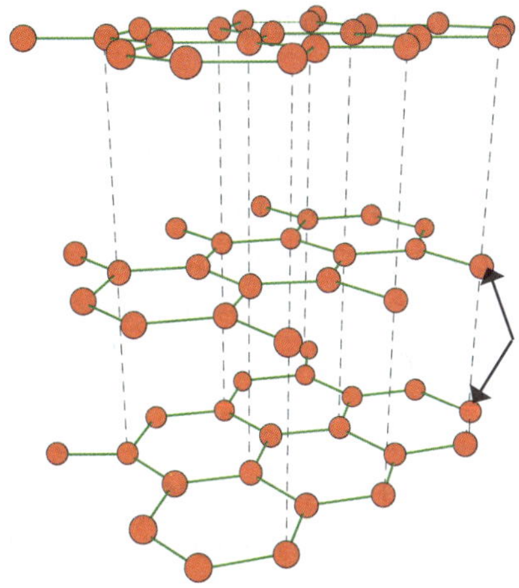

▲ Layered structure of graphite

Properties of Graphite

- Graphite is dark grey or black in colour and has a metallic lustre.
- It is opaque, soft and slippery to touch.
- It has a density of about 2.2 g/cm^3.
- It has a melting point of around 3700°C and hence, can withstand high temperatures.
- It is a good conductor of electricity and heat.
- When heated to about 700°C in air, graphite forms carbon dioxide.
- It is insoluble in most solvents and is slightly more chemically active than diamond.

Uses of Graphite

- It is used as electrodes in electric furnaces and electric cells.
- Due to its soft and slippery nature, graphite is widely used in machinery parts as a lubricant.
- It is used to make pencil leads.
- It is used in the manufacture of crucibles that are used to melt metals, as graphite is a good conductor of heat and has a high melting point.
- It is used as a moderator in nuclear reactors to slow down the speed of fast moving neutrons.
- It is used to make black paint and printer's ink because of its black colour and insoluble nature.

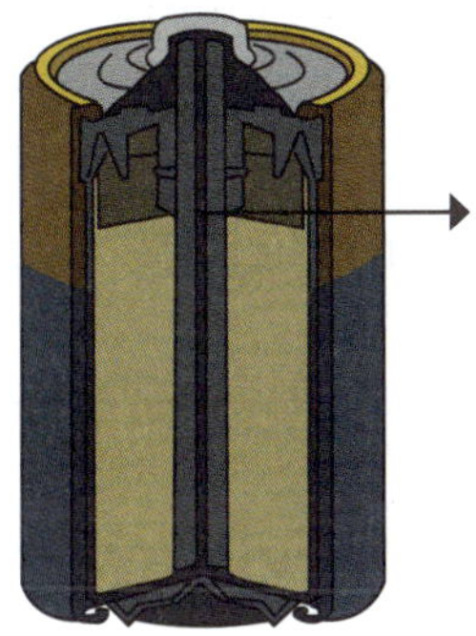

▲ Graphite rod as electrode in an electric cell

Fullerene

Fullerene is another crystalline allotrope of carbon, which has been discovered recently. The fullerene molecule, buckminsterfullerene (C_{60}), was discovered in the year 1985 collectively by the scientists Richard E. Smalley, Robert F. Curl, Sean O'Brien, James Heath and Harold Kroto.

The name 'buckminsterfullerene' was given to the fullerene molecule discovered as a homage to the American architect and scientist Buckminster Fuller. The geodesic dome buildings designed by him resemble the structure of buckminsterfullerene.

▲ Geodesic dome

Structure of Fullerene

Fullerene is the crystalline form of carbon with a large number of carbon atoms. The number of carbon atoms in the crystal structure of one molecule of fullerene can vary from 30 to 900. The arrangement of carbon atoms in fullerenes is in the form of hexagonal and pentagonal rings that are interlocked with each other.

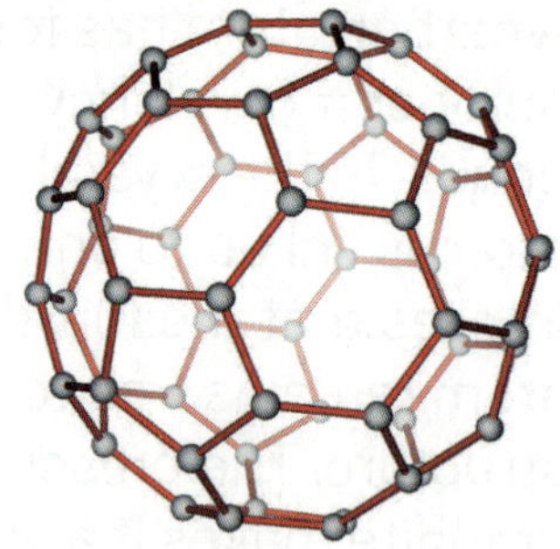
▲ Structure of spherical fullerene

Fullerenes can form a closed, cage-like structure (that is, a hollow sphere, known as **buckyballs**) or a cylindrical shape (known as carbon nanotubes or **buckytubes**).

The molecule of buckminsterfullerene is a spherical fullerene whose appearance is similar to a soccer ball (football). It consists of 60 carbon atoms and is represented with the molecular formula C_{60}.

Know the Scientists

Scientists Richard E. Smalley and Robert F. Curl, professors from Rice University, Texas, and Harold W. Kroto, from University of Sussex, England, collectively received the Nobel Prize in the year 1996 for the discovery of buckminsterfullerene. The three chemistry researchers worked with advanced spectrometers to study the molecular structure of carbon.

The discovery of fullerenes led to further research in the field of nanotechnology and electronics.

Richard E. Smalley

Robert Curl

Harold Kroto

Properties of Fullerenes

- Fullerenes are found in soot, interstellar dust (space between stars) and in carbon-rich rocks.
- They are bad conductors of electricity.
- They are magnetic in nature.
- They are odourless.
- They can be soluble in solvents like chloroform, benzene or toluene.

Uses of Fullerenes

- Fullerenes are used as lubricants.
- They are used as insulators.
- Some forms of fullerenes can conduct heat and electricity. So, they are used as superconductors and semiconductors.
- They are used in the process of drug delivery.

Revision Zone

Write T for True and F for False.

1. Carbon exists only in the combined state in nature.
2. Sulphur exhibits allotropy.
3. Diamonds are used in the manufacture of high precision thermometers.
4. The structure of buckminsterfullerene appears to be in the form of a soccer ball.
5. Graphite is used as a semiconductor.

Amorphous Forms of Carbon

Coal, charcoal, lampblack, gas carbon and coke are the amorphous forms of carbon. Out of these, only coal is the naturally formed amorphous form of carbon while the rest are man-made amorphous forms.

Coal

Coal is a black, hard, solid fossil fuel. It is formed when organic matter (mainly plants and trees) get deposited deep inside the earth and get decomposed under high pressure, high temperature and in the absence of air over a period of millions of years.

▲ Coal

There are different varieties of coal based on the carbon content. The different varieties of coal are anthracite, bituminous, sub-bituminous, lignite and peat. Anthracite is the best variety of coal having 92-98 per cent carbon content.

Uses of Coal

Coal has many significant uses.

- It is widely used as a fuel in industries and homes.
- It is used to make coal gas, coal tar and coke.
- It is used in power generation, production of steel, extraction of ores and manufacturing of cement.
- It is also used to prepare organic compounds like benzene and naphthalene, dyes, wax, fertilizers, shampoos, etc.

Charcoal

Charcoal is a black, soft and porous solid. It is prepared by heating organic substances like wood, bone and sugar at high temperatures in the absence of air or oxygen. Due to strong heating, the larger molecules of the organic substances break down into smaller molecules.

The process of breaking down of organic substances by heating them at high temperatures in the absence of air is called **destructive distillation**. During this process, the gases and liquids that have low boiling points are released into the air, leaving behind only charcoal as the residue.

Different Types of Charcoal

Based on the source that it is obtained from, charcoal is of different types: activated charcoal, wood charcoal, bone or animal charcoal and sugar charcoal.

Activated charcoal

Activated charcoal is also known as **activated carbon**. It is obtained from charcoal by heating it in the presence of hot gases resulting in the development of minute pores and internal spaces on it. This enhances the surface area resulting in its good adsorbing property.

Uses of activated charcoal

- It is widely used as a decolourizing agent.
- It is used in water purification systems to remove excess chlorine and odour from water.
- It is used in the purification of gold and extraction of metals.
- It is used in the medicinal field to treat poisoning.

Wood charcoal

Wood charcoal is prepared by the destructive distillation of wood in the absence of air. Wood shavings or saw dust are used for this. In this process, wood charcoal is left behind as a black, porous solid residue and gases like carbon dioxide, carbon monoxide, methane and hydrogen are produced. A mixture of these gases is combustible in nature and is called **wood gas**.

▲ Wood charcoal

Properties of wood charcoal

- It is black in colour, porous and brittle in nature.
- Because of its porous nature, wood charcoal can float on water.
- The porous nature of wood charcoal gives it a large surface area with less volume. Thus, it acts as a good adsorbent. **Adsorption** is the property of a substance due to which it can hold the molecules of solids, liquids or gases as a thin film or layer on its surface. The substance on whose surface adsorption takes place is called an **adsorbent**.
- It is a bad conductor of electricity and heat.

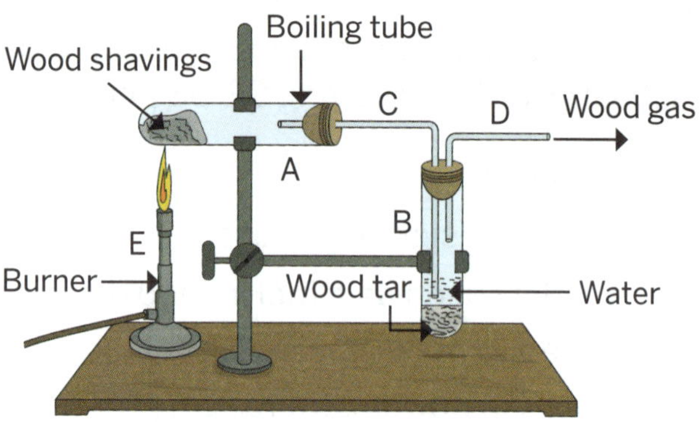

▲ Destructive distillation of wood

Uses of wood charcoal

- It is widely used as a fuel. It is considered a better fuel than wood as it is less polluting and releases more heat.
- It is used as a decolourizing agent in sugar solutions, petroleum products and alcohols due to its adsorbing nature. It can adsorb coloured substances on its surface.
- It is one of the important ingredients of gunpowder that is used as an explosive.
- It is used to make deodorants as it adsorbs foul-smelling gases.

- It is used in making gas masks for military and industrial purposes to remove poisonous gases from the air that is breathed in.
- It is used in the purification of water. It is used as an adsorbent in water filters and in water treatment plants to adsorb impurities and foul smell from water.

Bone or animal charcoal

Bone or animal charcoal is prepared by the destructive distillation of animal bones. The bones are first boiled in water to remove any fatty substances and then subjected to destructive distillation. It contains about 10-12 per cent carbon and the remaining amount contains calcium phosphate and calcium carbonate. Bone charcoal has good decolourizing property.

Uses of bone or animal charcoal

- It is widely used as a decolourizing agent, especially to decolourize sugar solutions as it removes the brown colour of raw sugar.
- It is used to manufacture phosphorus compounds.
- Ivory black (obtained by treating bone charcoal with hydrochloric acid) is used as a black pigment in paintings.
- It is used in the manufacture of white petroleum jelly and bone ash.

Sugar charcoal

Sugar charcoal is considered to be the purest form of amorphous carbon. It is a grey or black-coloured residue prepared by dehydrating cane sugar using concentrated sulphuric acid. It is also prepared by the destructive distillation of cane sugar.

Uses of sugar charcoal

- It is used as a decolourizing agent.
- It is used in the extraction of metals from their oxides by acting as a reducing agent.

Example:

$$\underset{\text{Lead Oxide}}{PbO} + \underset{\text{Sugar Charcoal}}{C} \longrightarrow \underset{\text{Lead}}{Pb} + \underset{\text{Carbon Monoxide}}{CO}$$

- It is used in the manufacture of artificial diamonds.

Lampblack

Lampblack is produced when hydrocarbons or carbon-rich substances such as oil, kerosene, petrol and wax are burned in a limited supply of air or oxygen. These substances burn with a smoky flame that contains free carbon. The free carbon produced during this process deposits as a fine black powder, which is referred to as lampblack. It consists of almost 99 per cent carbon. It is also called **carbon black** or **soot**.

In kerosene lamps, the soot that is formed along the walls of chimney is nothing but lampblack.

▲ Lampblack

Uses of Lampblack

- Lampblack is used in the preparation of black paints, printer's ink, black carbon paper and shoe polish.
- It is used in the manufacture of tyres.
- It is used to make gunpowder and *kajal*.

Activity 1

Aim: To prepare *kajal* at home from cooking oil, mustard oil or castor oil

Materials required: Wick made of cotton, cooking oil, mustard oil or castor oil, earthen lamp (*diya*), matchbox, steel boxes or vessels, copper plate

Procedure:

1. Take around 100 mℓ of cooking oil, mustard oil or castor oil in an earthen lamp.
2. Place the wick that is made of cotton into the oil.
3. Light the lamp with the help of a matchstick.
4. By using a few boxes or vessels, place the copper plate at some height over the lamp.
5. The position of the copper plate should be in such a way that the flame touches the inner surface of the copper plate. Observe what happens after sometime.

Preparation of *kajal*

Observation and conclusion: A black soot deposit is observed on the inner surface of the copper plate. This black soot is lampblack, which is widely used as *kajal* at home.

Gas Carbon

Gas carbon is produced by the destructive distillation of coal. It is also prepared by heating hydrocarbons at high temperatures in a closed container. Gas carbon deposits as a greyish substance on the inner walls of the container. It is a good conductor of electricity.

Uses of Gas Carbon

- It is used in the manufacture of electrodes.
- It is used as the carbon rod in arc lamps.

Coke

Coke is a hard, porous and grey-coloured substance obtained as a residue from the destructive distillation of coal. It contains about 95 per cent carbon and does not produce smoke on burning. It was first used by Chinese iron workers in the 9th century.

Uses of Coke

- Coke is used as a household and an industrial fuel. It is a non-polluting fuel.
- It is used in the extraction of metals by acting as a reducing agent.

- It is used in the manufacture of steel and iron.
- It is used in the production of water gas (composed of CO and H_2) and producer gas (composed of CO and N_2). Both are used as gaseous fuels.

Revision Zone

Match the amorphous form of carbon to its relevant use.

1. Wood charcoal	a. Electrodes
2. Animal charcoal	b. Black paint
3. Lampblack	c. Water gas
4. Gas carbon	d. Phosphorus compounds
5. Coke	e. Deodorant

Carbon Dioxide

Air contains around 0.03 per cent of carbon dioxide. It plays an important role as green plants prepare their food using carbon dioxide from air during photosynthesis.

Carbon dioxide was discovered by Von Helmont. He discovered the gas when he burned charcoal. The gas that was released did not support combustion. Later, in the year 1775, Joseph Black discovered carbon dioxide by treating calcium carbonate with dilute acids. Afterwards, Antoine Lavoisier named the gas as carbon dioxide.

Occurrence of Carbon Dioxide

Carbon dioxide can occur in the free state as well as in the combined state. In the free state, dioxide exists in the atmosphere. As carbon dioxide dissolves in water reasonably, it is present in the dissolved form in water bodies. It is also released during volcanic eruptions.

In the combined state, carbon dioxide is found in Earth's crust in the form of metallic bicarbonates and carbonates like calcium carbonate ($CaCO_3$) and magnesium carbonate ($MgCO_3$). It also occurs in sea shells and coral reefs.

Preparation of Carbon Dioxide

Laboratory Preparation of Carbon Dioxide

In the laboratory, carbon dioxide is prepared by reacting marble chips with dilute hydrochloric acid. Marble chips are mainly made of calcium carbonate.

In this reaction, calcium carbonate reacts with dilute hydrochloric acid to form calcium chloride, water and carbon dioxide.

$$\underset{\text{Calcium carbonate}}{CaCO_3} + \underset{\text{Hydrochloric acid}}{2HCl} \longrightarrow \underset{\text{Calcium chloride}}{CaCl_2} + \underset{\text{Water}}{H_2O} + \underset{\text{Carbon dioxide}}{CO_2}$$

Activity 2

Aim: To demonstrate the preparation of carbon dioxide from marble chips (calcium carbonate)

Materials required: Marble chips, dilute hydrochloric acid, round-bottomed flask, thistle funnel, beehive shelf, two-holed rubber cork, delivery tube and gas jar

Procedure: The apparatus for the experiment is set up as shown in the figure.

1. Some marble chips are taken in a round-bottomed flask.
2. Using the thistle funnel, dilute hydrochloric acid is added into the flask.
3. No heating is needed for the reaction to occur.

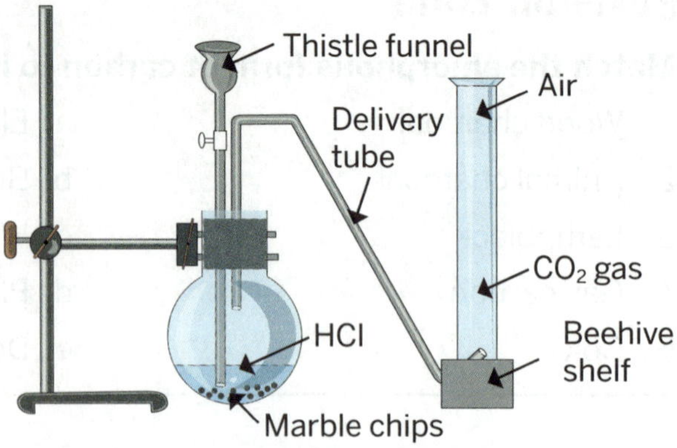

Observation: Calcium carbonate present in marble chips reacts with hydrochloric acid to form calcium chloride and water with the release of carbon dioxide gas. The gas released can be seen as bubbles in the flask. This gas passes through the delivery tube and gets collected in the inverted jar that is placed on the beehive shelf.

Conclusion: Carbon dioxide gas thus produced gets collected in the gas jar by the upward displacement of air as it is heavier than air.

Other Methods of Preparation of Carbon Dioxide

Carbon dioxide can also be prepared by the following methods.

- **Combustion**: When any compound containing carbon or hydrocarbon is burned in the presence of oxygen, it releases carbon dioxide.

$$\underset{\text{Carbon}}{C} + \underset{\text{Oxygen}}{O_2} \longrightarrow \underset{\text{Carbon dioxide}}{CO_2}$$

$$\underset{\text{Methane}}{CH_4} + \underset{\text{Oxygen}}{2O_2} \longrightarrow \underset{\text{Carbon dioxide}}{CO_2} + \underset{\text{Water}}{2H_2O}$$

> **Science in Context**
>
> When preparing carbon dioxide from marble chips, hydrochloric acid is preferred over sulphuric acid. This is because calcium carbonate reacts with sulphuric acid to form insoluble calcium sulphate. This forms a layer over the marble chips and stops further reaction.

- **Action of heat on metal carbonates and bicarbonates**: When metal carbonates and bicarbonates are heated, carbon dioxide is produced.

$$\underset{\text{Copper carbonate}}{CuCO_3} \xrightarrow{\text{Heat}} \underset{\text{Copper oxide}}{CuO} + \underset{\text{Carbon dioxide}}{CO_2}$$

$$\underset{\text{Sodium bicarbonate}}{2NaHCO_3} \xrightarrow{\text{Heat}} \underset{\text{Sodium carbonate}}{Na_2CO_3} + \underset{\text{Carbon dioxide}}{CO_2} + \underset{\text{Water}}{H_2O}$$

- **Action of acids on metal carbonates and bicarbonates**: Acids like hydrochloric acid, sulphuric acid and vinegar (acetic acid) react with metal carbonates and bicarbonates to release carbon dioxide.

$CaCO_3$	+	$2HCl$	$\longrightarrow$	$CaCl_2$	+	CO_2	+	H_2O
Calcium carbonate		Hydrochloric acid		Calcium chloride		Carbon dioxide		Water

$NaHCO_3$	+	CH_3COOH	$\longrightarrow$	CH_3COONa	+	CO_2	+	H_2O
Sodium bicarbonate		Acetic acid (Vinegar)		Sodium acetate		Carbon dioxide		Water

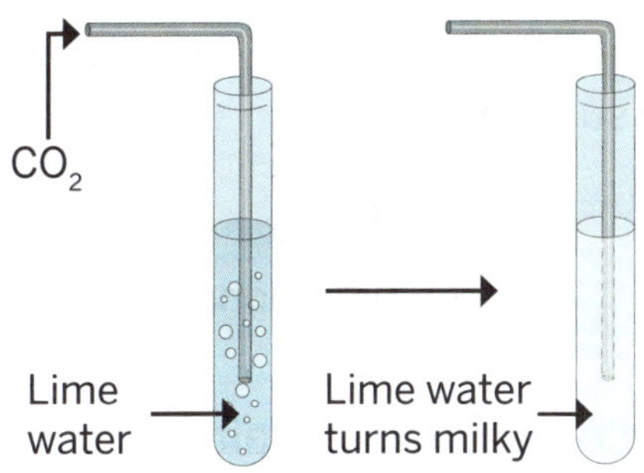

▲ Lime water test

Tests for Carbon Dioxide

The presence of carbon dioxide can be detected by two tests.

- **Lime water test**: If carbon dioxide is blown into a test tube containing lime water, it turns the lime water milky. Lime water is the other name for a dilute solution of calcium hydroxide. The calcium hydroxide reacts with carbon dioxide to form white, insoluble calcium carbonate. Thus, the lime water turns milky.
- **Burning matchstick test**: If a burning matchstick is introduced into a jar containing carbon dioxide, the matchstick extinguishes. This is because carbon dioxide does not support combustion.

Activity 3

Aim: To show that carbon dioxide does not support combustion

Materials required: Gas jar containing CO_2 and matchstick

Procedure: Light the matchstick and introduce it into the jar containing CO_2.

Observation: The matchstick extinguishes.

Conclusion: Carbon dioxide does not support combustion. Hence, the matchstick extinguishes.

Properties of Carbon Dioxide

Physical Properties

- Carbon dioxide is a colourless and odourless gas. It has a sour taste because of its acidic nature.
- It is heavier than air. Hence, it can be poured from one container to another like liquids.
- It is reasonably soluble in water. At high pressure, it dissolves in high quantity in water. Hence, it is dissolved in aerated drinks at high pressure.
- Carbon dioxide solidifies upon cooling at −78°C to form dry ice.

Chemical Properties

Carbon dioxide is also a chemically reactive gas. The following are its chemical properties.

- **Combustion**: Carbon dioxide does not support combustion and is itself a non-combustible gas. But metals like sodium, potassium and magnesium burn in the presence of carbon dioxide to form respective oxides and black specks of carbon.

$4K$	+	CO_2	$\longrightarrow$	$2K_2O$	+	C
Potassium		Carbon dioxide		Potassium oxide		Carbon (black specks)

- **Reaction with lime water**: Carbon dioxide reacts with lime water and turns it milky. However, when more carbon dioxide is passed through the milky solution, the calcium carbonate formed further reacts with carbon dioxide to form calcium bicarbonate, which is soluble in water. Hence, the solution becomes clear.

$Ca(OH)_2$	+	CO_2	$\longrightarrow$	$CaCO_3$	+	H_2O
Calcium hydroxide		Carbon dioxide		Calcium carbonate (Insoluble milky suspension)		Water

$CaCO_3$	+	CO_2	+	H_2O	$\longrightarrow$	$Ca(HCO_3)_2$
Calcium carbonate (Insoluble)		Carbon dioxide		Water		Calcium bicarbonate (Soluble)

- **Reaction with bases**: Carbon dioxide reacts with bases to form corresponding salts (carbonates) and water. Upon further reaction with more carbon dioxide, the corresponding bicarbonates are formed.

$2KOH$	+	CO_2	$\longrightarrow$	K_2CO_3	+	H_2O
Potassium hydroxide		Carbon dioxide		Potassium carbonate		Water

K_2CO_3	+	CO_2	+	H_2O	$\longrightarrow$	$2KHCO_3$
Potassium carbonate		Carbon dioxide		Water		Potassium bicarbonate

- **Reaction with water**: When carbon dioxide dissolves in water, it forms carbonic acid (a weak acid).

H_2O	+	CO_2	$\longrightarrow$	H_2CO_3
Water		Carbon dioxide		Carbonic acid

- **Reaction of carbon dioxide with litmus solution/paper:** Place a piece of moist blue litmus paper/blue litmus solution into the container that contains carbon dioxide gas. The litmus paper/litmus solution will turn from blue to red due to the acidic nature of carbon dioxide gas.

Uses of Carbon Dioxide in Everyday Life

Carbon dioxide is mainly used by plants in photosynthesis. It is also used in industries and bakeries. Some uses of carbon dioxide are as follows.

- **Photosynthesis**: Plants are the main source of food and oxygen for all living organisms on Earth. Green plants make use of carbon dioxide from the air to prepare their own food. In this process, carbon dioxide reacts with water in the presence of sunlight and chlorophyll to form glucose and oxygen. Hence, carbon dioxide is an essential gas for plants.

- **Baking industry**: In the preparation of bakery products like breads, cakes and pastries, baking soda (sodium bicarbonate) is added to the dough. Upon heating, it releases CO_2 within the dough in the form of bubbles, making the dough rise. As a result, cakes and breads become soft and fluffy in nature.

▲ Bakery product

- **Fire extinguishers**: Carbon dioxide does not support combustion and is heavier than air. Hence, it is used in fire extinguishers to put out fires. Carbon dioxide is stored in cylinders in liquefied form. When pressure is applied, the liquid form gets converted into the gaseous form. The carbon dioxide gas thus produced forms a layer over the fire and cuts off the supply of air (oxygen).
- **Aerated drinks**: In aerated drinks, CO_2 is dissolved in water under pressure. When the bottle is opened, CO_2 escapes from the drink with a fizz. At low temperatures, carbon dioxide dissolves in water at a higher rate.
- **Dry ice**: Solid carbon dioxide is called dry ice. It is obtained by cooling carbon dioxide to −78°C. Dry ice is used as a refrigerant to preserve food items like fruits, vegetables and meat. It is a sublimable substance and is non-toxic in nature. Unlike normal ice, dry ice does not melt into a liquid. It converts directly from its solid form to its gaseous form, that is, it sublimes. Hence, it is called dry ice.
- **Preparation of urea**: Urea is an important agricultural fertilizer. It is manufactured by the reaction of carbon dioxide with ammonia.
- **Medical uses**: Oxygen that is mixed with carbon dioxide is used in hospitals to support breathing in patients who have respiratory diseases like asthma and pneumonia.

▲ Dry ice

Carbon Monoxide

Properties of Carbon Monoxide

- It is a colourless, odourless gas and easily mixes with the air.
- It is a highly poisonous and flammable gas.
- It is slightly denser than air.
- It is soluble in benzene and ethanol but sparingly soluble in water.
- It is a neutral oxide.
- It forms carbon dioxide on burning in the presence of oxygen.

Sources of Carbon Monoxide

Carbon monoxide is one of the products obtained by the incomplete combustion (combustion that takes place in insufficient amount of oxygen).

It is formed when the carbon containing fuels burn in an insufficient amount of oxygen.

$$2C + O_2 \longrightarrow \underset{\text{Carbon monoxide}}{2CO}$$

The exhaust of motor vehicles and burning of fossil fuels are the main sources of carbon monoxide gas in the atmosphere. Volcanic eruptions are also one of the sources of CO in the atmosphere.

Carbon Monoxide Preparation in the Laboratory

- Carbon monoxide is produced by the dehydration process of formic acid with concentrated H_2SO_4.

$$\underset{\text{Formic acid}}{HCOOH} \xrightarrow{H_2SO_4} \underset{\text{Water}}{H_2O} + \underset{\text{Carbon monoxide}}{CO}$$

- By passing the carbon dioxide gas over heated carbon.

$$\underset{\text{Carbon dioxide}}{CO_2} + \underset{\text{Carbon}}{C} \longrightarrow \underset{\text{Carbon monoxide}}{2CO}$$

Uses of Carbon Monoxide

- It is extensively used as a fuel in the form of water gas and producer gas, thus known as industrial gas.
- It is a good reducing agent.

Carbon monoxide as a reducing agent in the extraction of iron: Carbon monoxide is a good reducing agent. It is a non-metal and forms gaseous non-metallic oxides on reaction with oxygen. Usually at high temperatures, being strong reducing agent by itself, carbon monoxide can remove oxygen from the metal oxides to form metals.

Carbon monoxide is used in the extraction process of iron. It reduces iron (III) oxide and results in the formation of iron and carbon dioxide.

$$\text{Iron (III) oxide + Carbon monoxide} \longrightarrow \text{Iron + Carbon dioxide}$$

$$Fe_2O_3(s) + 3CO\ (g) \longrightarrow 2Fe\ (l) + 3CO_2\ (g)$$

Harmful Properties of CO (Asphyxia)

Asphyxia is a medical condition in which the body does not get enough oxygen, which leads to death or coma if untreated.

Haemoglobin is a component present in the blood that carries oxygen to the various parts of the body.

When carbon monoxide is inhaled, it displaces oxygen and combines with the haemoglobin present in the blood to form carboxy-haemoglobin.

Carbon monoxide + Haemoglobin ⟶ Carboxy–haemoglobin

In case of carbon monoxide poisoning, carboxy-haemoglobin inhibits the reaction of haemoglobin with oxygen; thus, the tissues do not get enough oxygen and results in the death of a person due to suffocation. Hence, it is unsafe to sleep in a closed room that contains burning coal.

Precautions from CO Poisoning

- The first aid treatment for carbon monoxide poisoning is given by moving the affected person to a place that has fresh air
- By providing artificial respiration
- By taking medical assistance
- By ventilating the areas
- By removing the source of carbon monoxide from the affected area

Revision Zone

Fill in the blanks.

1. Carbon dioxide has a sour taste because of its ______________ (basic/acidic) nature.
2. Carbon monoxide is a ______________ (basic/neutral) oxide.
3. Carbon monoxide is a ______________ (toxic/ non-toxic) gas.
4. Asphyxia is a medical condition in which body does not get enough ______________ (CO/O_2).
5. Due to ______________ (oxidizing/reducing) property of CO, it is extensively used in the extraction process of iron.

Keywords

Allotropy: the property of an element to exist in various physical forms that have identical chemical properties but different physical properties

Crystals: solid substances in which the constituent ions, atoms or molecules are arranged in a regular, repetitive pattern with a definite shape in all dimensions

Fullerene: the crystalline form of carbon with a large number of carbon atoms; the number of carbon atoms can vary from 30 to 900

Hydrocarbons: organic compounds that are made up of only carbon and hydrogen atoms

Destructive distillation: the process of breaking down of organic substances by heating them at high temperatures in the absence of air

Asphyxia: a medical condition in which the body does not get enough oxygen, which leads to death or coma if untreated

In a Nutshell

- Carbon exists both in the free state and in the combined state in nature.
- Diamond, graphite and coal are the free forms of carbon.
- In the combined form, carbon exists as numerous compounds, such as carbon dioxide, cellulose, carbohydrates, proteins, fats, petroleum and natural gas.
- Carbon exists in two allotropic forms—crystalline and amorphous.
- Carbon atoms are arranged in a definite repeating order in the crystalline forms of carbon.
- In amorphous forms, carbon atoms are not arranged in any definite order.
- Diamond is the hardest naturally occurring substance on Earth.
- Naturally, diamonds are produced from carbon under high pressure and high temperature deep below the Earth's surface.
- Fullerene is a crystalline form of carbon containing a large number of carbon atoms arranged in the form of hexagonal or pentagonal rings.
- Charcoal is prepared in the absence of air or oxygen at high temperature by heating substances like wood, bone and sugar.
- Carbon dioxide is obtained when marble chips react with dilute hydrochloric acid.
- Carbon monoxide is a good reducing agent.

Exercise

1 Choose the correct answer for each of the following.

a. Identify the substance in which carbon exists in the free state.
   i. Cellulose ii. Graphite
   iii. Carbon dioxide iv. Petroleum

b. Identify the amorphous form of carbon.
   i. Graphite ii. Fullerene
   iii. Lampblack iv. Diamond

c. Identify the substance that is widely used as electrodes in batteries.
   i. Graphite ii. Coke
   iii. Lampblack iv. Wood charcoal

d. Identify the substance that is used to cut glass.
   i. Fullerene ii. Diamond
   iii. Gas carbon iv. Bone charcoal

e. Identify the naturally formed amorphous form of carbon from the following.
   i. Coal ii. Gas carbon
   iii. Coke iv. Lampblack

f. Which of the following is not a property of fullerenes?
   i. They are odourless.
   ii. They are magnetic in nature.
   iii. They are bad conductors of electricity.
   iv. They are soluble in water.

g. Wood charcoal is used in the
   i. purification of water
   ii. manufacture of tyres
   iii. cutting of glass
   iv. manufacture of coke

h. Which of these is not a property of carbon dioxide?
   i. Supports combustion
   ii. Acidic in nature
   iii. Colourless and odourless gas
   iv. Forms dry ice

2 Fill in the blanks.

a. The hardest known naturally occurring substance on Earth is __________ (fullerene/diamond).

b. Charcoal is __________ (a crystalline/an amorphous) form of carbon.

c. The substance used in the preparation of printer's ink is __________ (lampblack/coke).

d. __________ (Lampblack/Charcoal) is a good absorbent.

e. __________ (Wood charcoal/Sugar charcoal) is the purest form of amorphous carbon.

f. __________ (Carbon dioxide/Carbon monoxide) gas dissolves in water to form carbonic acid.

3 Write T for True and F for False.

a. Carbohydrates are combined forms of carbon.

b. Carbon exists in two allotropic forms.

c. Coke is also called as carbon black.

d. Graphite is a poor conductor of electricity.

e. Carbon monoxide prevents the blood from carrying oxygen in the body.

f. Wood charcoal can float on water.

g. Ivory black is used as a black pigment in paintings.

4 Define the following terms.

a. Allotropy

b. Fullerene

c. Destructive distillation

d. Adsorption

e. Asphyxia

5. **Differentiate between the following.**
   a. Organic compounds and inorganic compounds of carbon
   b. Natural diamonds and synthetic diamonds
   c. Coal and coke
   d. Wood charcoal and animal charcoal
   e. Charcoal and gas carbon

6. **Write the balanced equation for the following reactions.**
   a. Reaction of carbon monoxide with iron oxide
   b. Reaction of carbon dioxide with calcium carbonate
   c. Reaction of carbon dioxide with water

7. **Answer the following questions in brief.**
   a. Differentiate between amorphous and crystalline forms of carbon.
   b. Define allotropy. Give examples of elements that exhibit allotropy.
   c. Mention some of the uses of diamond.
   d. What happens when carbon burns in a limited supply of oxygen?
   e. Mention the various uses of sugar charcoal.
   f. What are the different varieties of coal?
   g. What is gas carbon?
   h. What are the combined states of carbon?
   i. Write the chemical equation for the reaction of calcium hydroxide with carbon dioxide.

8. **Answer the following questions in detail.**
   a. Explain any four amorphous forms of carbon.
   b. Distinguish between the structure of diamond and graphite.
   c. Briefly explain the chemical properties of carbon.
   d. List the chemical properties of carbon dioxide.
   e. Explain the tests done to detect the presence of carbon dioxide gas.
   f. Explain the properties and uses of carbon monoxide.

9. **Think and answer.**

   Ishita wanted to select one of the allotropic forms of carbon as a lubricant for fast moving machinery parts. Which material should she use and why?

   (Hint: Recall the structure and uses of crystalline forms of carbon.)

10. **Project**

   Take some chart papers and make game cards of various allotropic forms of carbon and their uses. Try to match the type of allotropic form of carbon to its relevant use.

11. **In the Library**

   - Collect information about conservation of non-renewable resources like coal and petroleum.
   - Collect information about destructive distillation of coal along with its uses. Prepare a chart on this and present this in your class.

Worksheet

Subject Integration

a. Ram slept in a closed room in which coal was burned. Will Ram be affected with asphyxia?

____

____

b. What is asphyxia? What precautions should Ram take to prevent himself from this condition?

____

____

____

____

c. What would be the product formed if Ram inhales more amount of carbon monoxide than oxygen?

Carbon monoxide + Haemoglobin ⟶ ____________________

d. Why is carbon dioxide preferred in fire extinguishers to put out fire in multi-storey hospitals?

____

____

____

____

Assessments

Assessment 1 (Chapters 1–4)

Maximum: 40

1 Choose the correct answer for each of the following. (5 × 1 = 5)

a. A substance that contains two or more substances mixed together is a ______.
   i. compound ii. mixture iii. element iv. molecule

b. The mass of an atom is determined by the sum of the masses of ______.
   i. electrons ii. neutrons iii. neutrons and protons
   iv. electrons and neutrons

c. Electrons were discovered by
   i. Bohr ii. Thomson iii. Dalton iv. Goldstein

d. Which of the following statement is correct?
   i. Mostly chemical changes are reversible
   ii. Volume is a chemical property of a substance
   iii. Rusting of iron is an example for physical change
   iv. A precipitate is the insoluble solid that forms during the chemical reaction

e. The law of conservation of mass states that matter cannot be
   i. changed or created ii. burned or destroyed
   iii. dissolved or disposed iv. created or destroyed

2 Fill in the blanks. (5 × 1 = 5)

a. The inter-particle space between the particles of ______ (gases/solids) is negligible.
b. The positively charged centre of an atom is called ______ (nucleus/proton).
c. Neutrons were discovered by ______ (Rutherford/Chadwick).
d. ______ (Sublimation/Evaporation) is a process of solids directly converting into gases.
e. ______ (Boiling of water/Baking a cake) is a physical change.

3 Write T for True and F for False. (5 × 1 = 5)

a. An element has two electrons in the M-shell. The atomic number of the element is 12.
b. Decantation is the best process for removing the tea leaves from tea.
c. The inter-particular force of attraction between the particles of gases is maximum.
d. Acid rain damaging a marble statue is a physical change.
e. The fixed circular paths around the nucleus are called orbits.

4 Give reasons for the following. (5 × 2 = 10)

a. Some elements exhibit variable valency.
b. Atom is electrically neutral.
c. The mass of the products formed is equal to the mass of the reactants.
d. Salt dissolved in water is an example of homogeneous mixture.
e. Gaseous particles have more compressibility.

5 Answer the following questions. (5 × 3 = 15)

a. Briefly explain Dalton's atomic theory.
b. What are the different indicators for a chemical change? Justify your answer.
c. Explain the discovery of electrons.
d. What are the different methods used to separate a solid–solid mixture? Explain any two.
e. Write the postulates of the kinetic theory of matter.

Assessment 2 (Chapters 5–9) **Maximum: 40**

1 Choose the correct answer for each of the following. (5 × 1 = 5)

a. Which among the following is the crystalline form of carbon that helps in the drilling of hard rocks and cutting of glass?
   i. Lampblack ii. Diamond iii. Graphite iv. Fullerene

b. Which of the following chemical reactions of hydrogen is also known as 'combustion'?
   i. Reaction of hydrogen with metals ii. Reaction of hydrogen with sulphur
   iii. Reaction of hydrogen with chlorine iv. Reaction of hydrogen with oxygen

c. The catalyst used in Bosch's process is ________ .
   i. copper oxide ii. iron oxide iii. calcium oxide iv. sodium oxide

d. Identify the chemical formula of calcium hydroxide.
   i. CaOH ii. $Ca(OH)_2$ iii. Ca_2OH iv. $(Ca)_2OH$

e. The reaction $AgNO_3 + NaCl \longrightarrow AgCl + NaNO_3$ is an example of a
   i. combination reaction ii. displacement reaction
   iii. decomposition reaction iv. double displacement reaction

2 Fill in the blanks. (5 × 1 = 5)

a. The naturally formed amorphous form of carbon is ________ (coal/lampblack).

b. The substance that is widely used as electrodes in electric cells is ________ (graphite/coke).

c. The composition of water gas is ________ ($CO + H_2$/$CO + N_2$).

d. The process of addition of hydrogen to a substance is ________ (oxidation/reduction).

e. The substance present in larger component in the solution is known as ________ . (solute/solvent)

3 Write T for True and F for False. (5 × 1 = 5)

a. The purity of diamonds is measured in joules.

b. Hydrogen gas is acidic in nature.

c. Liquid hydrogen is used as a rocket fuel.

d. Pure water is a good conductor of electricity.

e. Al_2O_3 is an example of a neutral oxide.

4 Give reasons for the following. (5 × 2 = 10)

a. Graphite is soft and slippery in nature.

b. Carbon is widely used in the extraction of metals.

c. Hydrogen acts as both an oxidizing agent and a reducing agent.

d. Zinc oxide (ZnO) does not show any colour change with litmus paper.

e. Permanent hardness of water cannot be removed by boiling.

5 Answer the following questions. (5 × 3 = 15)

a. Explain the chemical properties of hydrogen.

b. List the different properties of water. Explain any five.

c. Distinguish between the structure of diamond and graphite.

d. Write a short note on decomposition reaction and its types.

e. What are the steps involved in balancing a chemical equation? Explain with examples.

NOTES